Just Keep Going

*Spiritual Encouragement from the
Mom of a Troubled Teen*

Sarah H. Nielsen

Just Keep Going
by Sarah H. Nielsen

Printed in the United States of America

ISBN 9781606474495

Unless otherwise indicated, Bible quotations are taken from New American Standard Bible. Copyright © 1973 by The Lockman Foundation.

www.xulonpress.com

Table of Contents

Acknowledgments

On summer evenings, I would lace up my walking shoes, grab my music and headphones, my reflector wrist band and tissues, and set out in the darkness of the neighborhood to pray, cry, mourn and beg God for help, as I watched one of our three sons spiral down through his teenage years in a distress that I could never have imagined. At night, no one would see my tears or hear me groan, struggling for words that could accurately express the fear in my heart and the desperation I felt for God to intervene. The promises of God which I heard in the songs those nights brought me peace.

I asked God to provide as a companion another mom in the same situation to pray with, share the pain and divide the grief. I did not find her. He did give me good books, a counselor, encouraging friends and my mother, who was wise enough to love her grandson for what she knew was inside him. He gave me a strong husband to do the hard and scary parenting, and who reminded me of the good when I only saw the bad. Still, I never had another mom in my same place with whom to talk or pray. As a result, I experienced and understood God's love and care for me in a way I never had before. For that, of course, I am tremendously thankful.

I hope that this book will be a friend to you. I hope that it will be a place you can go to remember that you are not doing this alone. I pray that God will give you what you need, when you need it. I know how much He wants to do so, and that He can. I am confident that He will.

Thank you loyal, patient brothers John and Peter. Thank you Mom, Ted, René, Andrea, Cindy, Susie, Pam, Mary, Elizabeth, Sandy, Betsy, Jill, Courtney, Caitie, Jane, Ian, Toby, Tracy, Annie, Nate, Drew, Ryan, Craig, Gary, Becky, Burnie, Suzy, my Moms in Touch group, Epikos Church, Mugisha Dianne and many others. All of you asked questions, listened, cared, encouraged, offered wisdom and prayed what accumulated into a vast mountain range of prayers for Ted.

Thank you to all the people whose names I don't know who prayed for Ted. One day both of us will thank you face to face.

Thank you to my husband Bush, the greatest encourager this side of heaven. Our little Teddy was accurate when he used to whisper in your ear before going to sleep, "you're the best dad." You are also the best editor.

Thank you Ted, for the freedom to publish this book. Cherished son, welcome back.

God, thank You.

Introduction

I wrote this book based on ten years of journal entries chronicling the heartache of watching our son, Ted, slip away from our family and walk into the welcoming arms of what turned out to be drug and alcohol addiction. In the margins of my spiral notebooks filled with writings from my morning times with God, I would occasionally put an asterisk next to a revelation or discovery that God gave in that moment to encourage me. My times in God's Word adjusted my thinking, comforted me and equipped me to continue trusting God, one day at a time. With the not-so-gentle prodding of my husband, I expanded on those entries, in order to pass on what I had learned to other mothers who were suffering as I was. I know you are out there.

For a while, I put the book aside as our ten-year struggle with Ted intensified and I resolved to pay as much attention as possible to homeschooling our youngest son in his eighth grade year.

On my 52nd birthday, September 30, 2008, I retrieved Ted from a week in an alcohol and drug detox hospital unit and checked him into what turned into six months in residential treatment. Less than an hour later that day, I led the first meeting of a church Bible Study with ten women I had never met. Life goes on.

And so your life goes on. You zombie out of bed with this child on your mind, go to work or stay home and manage other children, all the while leaking tears from eye and heart. Alone in the privacy of your car, you whisper or maybe shout to God or into the air, "I don't know what to do. I don't know what to do."

As mothers, we advocate for our children. We kiss boo-boos, cheer them on from the bleachers and encourage them at the kitchen table. We celebrate their victories and console them on their failures. We defend them, brag about them to our own mothers, and occasionally deliver a school assignment forgotten on the bedroom floor. When their spirits leave their connection to ours to pursue a substance, person, lifestyle or seduction, we may eventually find that there is nothing we can do to fix this situation. We learn to pray.

Perhaps you are walking a very lonely path, as I did. Maybe this book will help your peripheral vision to see that God Himself is walking that path next to you, in front of you, behind you, with His hand on your shoulder saying, "This is the way, walk in it."

Sarah Nielsen
February 16, 2011

Day 1. First Responder

"But as for me, I would seek God, and I would place my cause before God, who does great and unsearchable things, wonders without number. ...He sets on high those who are lowly, and those who mourn are lifted to safety."

Job 5:8-9, 11

The above verse is found on a water-stained Bible verse-of-the-day page that, for three years, has been perched on the windowsill above my kitchen sink. It is a one-item to-do list: go first to God. Don't make a phone call. Don't write an email. Don't corner your husband. Apprehend Jesus. He is flexed for the tackle.

I'm not sure what this might look like for you. For me, those alarming times might find me kneeling over the seat cushion of my living room chair with a box of Kleenex by my side. I might be flinging myself face down on my bed to tell God how mad, hurt, scared, embarrassed or freaked out I am. Sometimes, it means that I grab my headphones and CD player and run out the door to be alone with Him. I pretend to mouth the words of songs as I walk by neighbors, but really I am telling God, "I'm afraid, I'm afraid, I'm afraid." God keeps up with me and I can almost hear Him saying between my breaths, "I know. I'm right here. Talk to Me."

When I let Jesus be my first responder, I am calm enough afterward to call a friend, but by then I usually already have what I need. The adrenaline drains and my heart slows down. I regain some perspective and my head clears. He gives me the necessary courage to take any next steps, or the peace to let it be. I can make the conscious choice to go to God first, or I can avoid Him and stay needy. Who else can simultaneously talk me down and do crisis management on the tsunami in my head? Only He understands the truth of the circumstance and the people involved.

Our loved ones can encourage us, but they can't really *do* much. At times I have offered up information which they were better off not knowing. I imagine our patient God, watching me frantically grab the phone for my husband and best friends while He waits for the help line to shorten. Have you noticed how often you can't get through to the friend? "Thus says the Lord who made the earth, the Lord who formed it to establish it, the Lord is His name, 'Call to Me, and I will answer you, and I will tell you great and mighty things, which you do not know."[1]

We have a sweet example in the story of Hannah in 1 Samuel, Chapter 1. She couldn't get pregnant and her husband's mean other wife wouldn't let her forget it. Finally, she broke down sobbing. In her explanation to a man observing and judging her, she cried that -- if he must know -- she wasn't drunk; she was telling God her problems. When she was done crying she got up, ate something -- Oreos? -- probably washed her face, re-applied her base make-up and put on a brave countenance, as we women are prone to do. Eventually she got the baby she craved, but in the meantime God was more than willing to listen to her issues while answering her prayer.

Fifteenth century author Baltasar Gracián wrote, "The wise does at once what the fool does at last." Go to Him, call on Him, sob to Him, yell to Him, and even argue with Him. He can take it. Try all other means first to help yourself if you must -- I have. Then reach out for real help and take the extended hand of God.

Thank You, Lord that You are available whenever I need to talk, cry, question or explode. Thank You that, when I leave the calmness of Your presence, I can also leave my cause with You, knowing that You will do the great, the miraculous, the marvelous or just simply the helpful.

Lord, I pray that You would remind me to go to You first. No stoic bucking up, no detours for me. You can take brute honesty and a whole lot of uninterrupted sobbing. You're the Father; I'm the child. I'm rolling my wheelbarrow of heartache and confusion over to You. I can hardly believe that You want it, but You do.

Day 2. Whose Child Is This Anyway?

"Faithful is He who calls you, and He also will bring it to pass."
1 Thessalonians 5:24

Do you ever think that you are the wrong parent for your teen? Do you suspect that God got interrupted by a phone call and lost track of where He was when He put you together? When we were in the car or at the dinner table, just the two of us, neither my son Ted nor I could think of anything to say or ask in the thick tension of our relationship. When we were arguing and he told me I made him crazy, I would think (and sometimes say) "oh, yeah, I know exactly how you feel." Later I would tell God, "Somebody was switched at birth because I am not the right mom for this kid. What I do bugs him. He bristles at what I say. Everything I am seems to be nails on his chalkboard."

The irony is that Ted and I are very much alike. We are like the positive end of a battery up against the positive end of another battery. The truth that it was God who made me his mom makes me cling to the above verse. I am right for the job; in fact, I am perfect for the job. I need to let God do the job through me. I think it means that difficult interactions between our children and us require a lightning flash prayer to God for help. We ask before we speak or act; we listen and we think it through. I have opted for silence in situations where I felt explosive but was unsure of the right words. I asked and waited -- sometimes not in that order -- for the right words from a proper perspective. My wise friend Cindy told me a very long time ago that you can almost always come back to a person and add more: "You know, I was thinking about what you said…" You can't, however, take back what you have already let out.

God put this little person, this child, in my arms umpteen years ago. Back then, we both felt that we were made for each other, and we were. Some things in the last decade have tempted me to think otherwise, but my first instincts were right. We are the right mothers for our children. If you can't see it, just choose to believe it. God knows we are not fully equipped in our humanness to do or be it all, so He says He will. He is

5

faithful to what He has given you, to what He has called you, and He will do it.

My just-like-me son is in his second year of college now. On my 50th birthday he wrote this: "I love you so much. I couldn't ask for a more wonderful mom." I don't tell you that to brag or make you feel bad that your own teen went out the door this morning with a grunt or worse. I have had many of those mornings. However, things can change. This teenage statue of icy granite, planted in a messy bedroom with the door closed, can transform into flesh and blood. Anything is possible when you get God involved.

Thank You, Lord, that I am the parent of this child. You chose me to be his parent because it is in Your plan. Therefore, I will not question Your decision that I am right where I should be. Having said that, Lord, thank You for the promise "Faithful is He that calls you, and He will do it," because so often I can't.

Lord, I pray that I will allow You to raise this child with me. I am your choice for the task but I am inadequate. You don't call the equipped, You equip the called. Show me how to do this work.

Day 3. Truth – Get Some

"Buy the truth and do not sell it; get wisdom, discipline and understanding."

Proverbs 23:23

The feeling is like a punch in the stomach and a sudden twist to the heart -- discovering pieces of paper, computer screens, items in the car or backpack, bits of uncovered information I wish I didn't have to know. Phone calls from school and the mother of our son's friend left me stunned with upsetting information about our son's doings. I paced my kitchen, clenching my hands and wiping my tear-wetted face. Similarly, another mom told me that, after taking yet another call from the principal about her son's infractions, she screamed words of frustration in her empty house until she fell on her bed, hoarse and exhausted.

These are times when we are allowed to see truth. It is not welcome, but it is necessary. Have you felt like I have -- possibly in a time of relative calm -- that there was trouble in the air? I took a walk one afternoon and said to God, "I know there is something going on that I need to know, Lord. I feel it. I wasn't ready to know it yesterday but I think I can handle it today. Show me some truth."

These are prayers that are not dissimilar to those in which we ask for patience. The words stick in my throat, but I know I need to say them. I want what is necessary but I want it to happen gently. This is not always possible. Truth allows us to understand more of what we are dealing with in our child's world. If the truth is bad, God will be in the middle of it, giving wisdom and direction. Sometimes the truth turns out to be much less awful than we had imagined. Sometimes, though, it is worse.

Although I have been guilty of denial, I have tried to learn that my assumptions can be just plain wrong. If I say "my child would NEVER" do something, or that "my child ALWAYS" does something else, I exhibit naiveté about human nature and the ability that each of us has to cross a boundary.

7

I have told my children how I consistently pray that they will be caught in the things they do wrong. They marvel at how it comes to pass that, while others move under the radar, they are discovered. It is better, I believe, to reveal issues as they happen than after they accumulate or escalate, although this is not always how life unfolds.

I don't like praying for truth. It is scary, but I guess I would rather know my leg is broken and get it set than to walk on it and make it worse. Asking for truth is like asking for a blinding spotlight in a sleepy darkness but, if we expect to live in reality, turn on the lights. God will walk with us.

Thank You, Lord, that You entrust me with the truth I am capable of knowing. I can handle what You show me because, if I press into You, I will find the strength. Thank You for monitoring when and how I know truth according to Your love and tender care for me.

Lord, I pray for maturity and courage to deal wisely with what comes my way. As I am able to know it, show truth to me and give me calm and wisdom in my next steps. Infuse me with discernment, maturity, understanding and, as always, love.

Day 4. Hidden Treasures

"'For I know the plans I have for you, declares the Lord, plans for welfare and not for calamity to give you a future and a hope. Then you will call upon Me and come and pray to Me, and I will listen to you, and you will seek Me and find Me, when you search for Me with all your heart."

Jeremiah 29:11-13

Not a few mothers in your church, your school, work or clubs share a secret pain about their children which they internalize. In many communities, it is not politically correct to admit that your student is not and has never been in any honors program, been given the lead (or any other part) in the school play, and will not be giving the valedictory speech at graduation. Some of us are just hoping that our children graduate at all, so we are quiet.

We live in a culture that measures students in terms of their academic success and notable accomplishments. It is easy to value a child in numerical terms: class rank, ACT/SAT score or grade point average.

We know that each child is so much more than his or her measurable achievements, but we stand in a forlorn place. No one realizes better than us the inner gifts our child possesses that do not appear on a report card or high school résumé. We are intensely proud of the people we know our children to be inside, but the world demands proof on paper.

We may fall silent at a parent party full of achievement chatter, but we can always talk to God. He embraces the best in our children. He sees through their rebellion to the raw beauty He gave them before they were born. We are welcomed on our knees any time, to discuss our children with their Creator and biggest fan.

The old poem below does not lose its potency with the years. Mothers' hearts are the same toward their children now as they have always been. The relentless will of a mother to reclaim her child is fueled by a God who wills the same. He wants them back because they are pearls of great worth.

Mother's Elbows on My Bed

I was but a youth and thoughtless, as all youths are
apt to be;
Though I had a Christian mother who had taught me
carefully,
There came a time when pleasure of the world came
to allure,
And I no more sought the guidance of her love so
good and pure.

Her tender admonitions fell but lightly on my ear,
And for the gentle warnings I felt an inward sneer.
How could I prove my manhood, were I not firm of
will?
No threat of future evil, should all my pleasure kill.

But mother would not yield her boy to Satan's sinful
sway,
And though I spurned her counsel, she knew a better
way.
No more she tried to caution, of ways she knew were
vain,
And though I guessed her heartache, I could not
know its pain.

She made my room an altar, a place of secret prayer,
And there she took her burden, and left it in His care.
And morning, noon and evening by that humble
bedside low,
She sought the aid of Him Who best can understand a
mother's woe.

And I went my way unheeding, careless of the life I
led,
Until one day I noticed prints of elbows on my bed.
Then I saw that she had been there, praying for her
wayward boy,
Who for love of worldly pleasure, would her peace of
mind destroy?

While I wrestled with my conscience, Mother
wrestled still in prayer,

Till that little room seemed hallowed, because so oft
she met Him there.
With her God she held the fortress, and though not a
word she said,
My stubborn heart was broken by those imprints on
my bed.

Long the conflict raged within me, sin against my
mother's prayers.
Sin must yield – for Mother never wavered while she
daily met Him there.
And her constant love and patience were like coals
upon my head,
Together with the imprints of her elbows on my bed.

Mother-love and God-love are a combination rare,
And one that can't be beaten when sealed by earnest
prayer.
And so at last the fight was won, and I to Christ was
led,
And Mother's prayers were answered by her elbows
on my bed.
                                        -- Unknown

Thank You, Lord, that even though most often I can't *do* anything to
change the heart of my child, I can pray for him and ask You to work.
This is not the least I can do – it is the best. What would this road be
like if I could not go to You with what is on my heart and my mind?
Lord, I pray with my elbows on my son's bed. I bend the knee to You
who can only change him to want a life that is bursting with all that
You have for him. Give my child a thirst and hunger for righteousness
and for You. Let him feel the emptiness and ask You to fill it.

Day 5. Which Day?

**"For ye have need of patience that, after ye have done the will of
God, ye might receive the promise."**

Hebrews 10:36 KJV

With my coat still on after a girls' night out, I stand at the kitchen
sink, my arms on the counter, my head bowed. On the way home I had
spoken with God about what triggered my concerns about Ted's
chronic state of unhappiness and angst. His problems twist my heart
even at 11 o'clock this night. "When, God?" I ask again. "When will
this end?"

I glance at my Bible verse-a-day calendar. Today's verse is "For ye
have need of patience that, after ye have done the will of God, ye might
receive the promise." Oh, yes, I have need of patience.

What is the will of God that I might do in the meantime? It is, I
think, to pray. It is to live my life in the best obedience I can perform
in line with His Word -- His Word which lifts my head in the late-night
darkness at my kitchen counter. My impatience in the time that passes
during which my prayers appear to be unanswered is inconsequential.
God Himself made the time, the lifetime, the child. He will unfold the
plan as it should be, not the least bit intimidated by me staring at Him,
arms crossed and foot tapping.

I agree that I have need of patience. I don't have it. Give it to me,
God. Give me what I need to enable me to wait. Fascinated by God's
conversation with me through my little daily Bible verse calendar, I
cheat and flip the page to the next day, which tells me "Those who wait
upon the Lord will renew their strength. They will mount up on wings
like eagles. They will walk and not grow faint. They will run and not
become weary."[2] Well okay then, load me up with strength as I wait
with confidence in a timekeeper who has never missed a cue in my own
life. I will wait upon the Lord, not upon the clock.

I heard a new song that I love and I make it my prayer – altering the
meaning slightly to fit my purposes. It speaks of the one day in eternity

12

after Jesus returns, but I ask God to make it the day on which our son will say yes to Him.

> One day voices that lie will all be silenced. One day all that's divided will be made whole again.
> One day death will retreat and wave its white flag. One day.
> Come quickly, we want to see Your glory, every knee bowed down before Thee.
> Every tongue offers you praise, with every hand raised,
> Singing glory to You and unto You only, we sing glory to Your name.
> We know not the day or the hour, or the moments in between.
> But we know the end of the story and we'll see…Your glory.[3]

Thank You, Lord, that my cause is not on the back burner of Your will. You are allowing and even doing what is necessary for the outcome You desire. My wait is not without purpose. It is interwoven with Your plan for my child's life as well. I have a hard time waiting. Thank You for offering to help.

Lord, I pray to see Your glory. Come quickly, even into this life circumstance, and bring Your kingdom into it just like it is in heaven. I accept Your offer to strengthen me as I wait. Make the waiting count, God, as I in the meantime try to do Your will.

Day 6. Herculean Hope

Every few months, my former college roommate Cindy and I meet halfway between our homes, which are two hours apart. We always eat at the same restaurant, order the same thing, split a blonde brownie a la mode for dessert and talk for at least three hours. We catch up, but mostly we gird up to know what and how to pray for one another until we meet again. The morning after one of our lunches, Cindy sent me this email:

> "I prayed all the way home and into the night. I found some awesome verses this morning. I hope they encourage you like they did me and I am claiming them on your behalf. First, for you...'May the God of hope fill you with all joy and peace as you trust in Him, so that you may overflow with hope by the power of the Holy Spirit.' Romans 15:13. For Ted, Isaiah 64:1-5a 'O that Thou wouldst render the heavens and come down, that the mountains might quake at Thy presence – as fire kindles the brushwood, as fire causes water to boil – to make Thy name known to [Ted] that [Ted] may tremble at Thy presence! For from of old they have not heard nor perceived by ear, neither has the eye seen a God besides Thee Who acts in behalf of the one who waits for Him, Thou dost meet him who rejoices in doing righteousness, who remembers Thee in Thy ways." I believe that God is working every day! Love you so, Cindy."

Cindy knows that, when we have hope for our children, it is not the same as daydreaming. Our hope is not superstition. It is not mere positive thinking or optimism. We don't have to be afraid that we will be disappointed. God has the ability to fill you with joy and peace – the result of hopefulness – even while you are still hoping. Hope trusts Him and we have every right to do that – in fact, He asks us to. Hope is not a placebo that God prescribes to make us feel better. We will

OVERFLOW with hope, by the power of the Holy Spirit rising inside us. I sometimes call it wishing. I don't care if that's proper Christian talk – it makes me feel as secure as a little child who tells her dad what she wants.

Hope has a body. It's real, not a fantasy, that God prescribes as a therapeutic antidote to worrying. It results in something. Cindy's prayer for Ted made me see what God is capable of doing. This is real power coming down from heaven and quaking mountains, lighting fires and making overconfident teens tremble. These verses in Isaiah tell me that nothing is greater than He who moves heaven and earth on behalf of a waiting, obedient mom and for His own glory.

When circumstances with Ted go from bad to worse and my hope wanes, I think about the people like Cindy who are praying. I might not see any apparent change at the moment, but I know there is a storage room of prayers in heaven as big as a stadium with my son's name on it. I hope for the day when God says "open the door."

Thank You, Lord, that while hope may be childlike, it is not childish. You not only encourage hope, You define Yourself by it. Thank You that, if I don't find a shred of good news for this day, Your Word gives me permission to hope – with confidence.

Lord, I pray that You will give hope to me when I can't cultivate it. Will You remind me that I can and should have hope? Make Yourself huge to my child, that he may tremble at Your presence. In the meantime, I'll wait for You. I'll try to reflect you in all my ways.

Day 7. Who Knew?

"And not only this, but we also exult in our tribulations, knowing that tribulation brings about perseverance; and perseverance, proven character; and proven character, hope; and hope does not disappoint, because the love of God has been poured out within our hearts through the Holy Spirit who was given to us."

Romans 5:3-5

Do you know that God is huge on perseverance? The simple fact that you are hanging in makes God proud of you. I can be spent, out of tears, without an idea or agenda, but if I can say, "Well God, I'm still standing, putting one foot in front of the other," I make God happy. I may not be able to do much more, but I can do that. After I sent her a discouraged email, my friend responded with what she said God seemingly whispered in her ear at a particularly low moment in her life: "He seemed to be telling me" she said, 'Just keep going.'"

This last week, I had lunch with a woman whose children are now grown and out of the house. We had wanted to get together ever since we had a brief mind-sharing conversation at a rummage sale one summer morning. Over salads this day, we told things about our lives, first in small talk, then in more detail. She recounted the difficult years she spent with a son in rebellion. It was a decade ago, but still her voice quieted and her face sobered when she told me about one moment of extreme heartache and frustration. "I hate this and I can't do this one more second," she remembered screaming to God over and over again. "Get me out of here. I don't want to do this anymore. This is not what I signed up for and I'm getting out!"

My new friend and I sat for a moment, looking silently at each other with tearful eyes, reliving these feelings we have both known. We agreed that, in those moments in the pit of despair, we had felt the impulse to get in the car and leave everything – even the other children and our beloved husbands – and keep driving until we reached a place that looked unlike our real lives. There we would read stacks of books that have nothing to do with parenting, sleep a lot, shop and over-buy,

16

and pretend we were someone else from somewhere else. She never did it. Even after ranting through the house until her head ached and the tears dried on her face, she knew she had to "just keep going."

I'm often not sure what, other than God's magnetic force, kept me from emigrating to Canada in times of desperation or exasperation. I knew that I loved our son so fiercely that, by pure stubbornness, I was going to see this through. But I have felt so incredibly sick of it that I *wanted* to check out. "No," God was saying to my heart, "you can do this. Just keep going."

Perseverance is valued by God. In a way, it is a form of faith. You keep going with Him out of sheer obedience, perhaps, but isn't that what Jesus did? We know He wanted to escape the cross, but to Jesus it was not about His own will in the moment, but God's plan for eternity. Perseverance has a purpose.

Thank You, Lord, for acknowledging that I am still in the game. You are a God who knows that at times all I can do is show up but, because I love You and I love my child, I will persevere with the knowledge that You are building something in me.

Lord, I pray that You, who are my friend, would please give me whatever it is I need to keep going this day and in hard days to come. I want You to deliver me from all of this but, in the end, I want to see this through even more. Please give me the character You promise for simply hanging in.

Day 8. Looking Up From the Bottom

"Though the fig tree should not blossom, and there be no fruit on the vines, though the yield of the olive should fail, and the fields produce no food, though the flock should be cut off from the fold, and there be no cattle in the stalls, Yet I will exult in the Lord, I will rejoice in the God of my salvation."

Habakkuk 3:17, 18

On difficult days, I would go off on my walk with my music and listen to a heartrending song over and over again. Why do we drift to sad songs when we're sad? Maybe it is comforting to know that we are not alone in our specific pain. Somewhere, a lyricist has understood my struggle and put words to it. How often I have used lyrics to express to God what I could not articulate on my own.

Maybe songs open up the reservoir of tears that we have stoically suppressed that day. Various Christian songwriters gave me a voice. They put into lyrics what I wanted to say to God and, at other times, what He was saying to me. Because I walked during the dark, my tear-stained face was veiled, and I felt the freedom to mouth desperate words of frustration.

On my regular walking route, relief would come when I rounded a particular corner and reached the top of a certain hill in the neighborhood. As I would look up in the vastness of the sky, I would see all that God was capable of creating. If He could make galaxies, surely He could do something significant in the life of one teenage boy in Wisconsin. It was then that my CD would reach the song, *Holy, Holy, Holy.* The greatest comfort to me was to think of how vast my God is. The more I know Him and the further I get in my relationship with Him, the more I see Him work and the more confident I am in handing to Him the care of our son.

Pain must always be partnered with praise. I would not end a walk without praise because, no matter how I feel, God is still God and deserves my praise. On that same CD, singer Fernando Ortega shares these words:

18

When the morning falls on the farthest hill, I will sing
His name; I will praise Him, still.
When dark trials come and my heart is filled, with the
weight of doubt, I will praise Him, still.
For the Lord our God, He is strong to save, from the
arms of death, from the deepest grave.
And He gave us life in His perfect will, and by His
good grace I will praise Him, still. [4]

My mother says "everything will be better in the end and, if it is not better, it is not the end." There are times to cry while we wait, but we must also praise. When we look back at His faithfulness in our past, we know He is worthy of our praise no matter how desperate the situation. Even in the dark night, there is light above. Look up.

Thank You, Lord, that I am not the only one who feels despair about a child. Not all of Your children followed You either. But You are more vast than the sky. You are bigger than our problems and deeper than our sadness. Thank You for the majesty and beauty of nature as a reminder of Your power, Your authority and Your great love for me.
Lord, I pray that You will make me a hopeful person. Make me someone who gives hope to others because I genuinely believe that You will show Yourself glorious one day in my situation. What You have done for me now is enough, but I know it is not all. I praise you still for who You are.

Day 9. Lifeguard or Puppy?

"But now, thus says the Lord, your creator, O Jacob, and He who formed you, O Israel, 'Do not fear, for I have redeemed you; I have called you by name; you are Mine! When you pass through the waters, I will be with you; And through the rivers, they will not overflow you. When you walk through the fire, you will not be scorched, nor will the flame burn you. ...Do not fear, for I am with you.'"

Isaiah 43:1-2, 5a

Working out my aggravation through exercise, I ran forcefully on my treadmill, roughly wiping away dripping tears and flinging them with anger. "Thanks a lot, God," I said out loud to Him, with sarcasm. "Thanks a lot for being with me in all this. What good does that do? I don't really need someone to be with me, I need someone to fix this. I need someone to DO SOMETHING!"

I was thinking of God as my puppy. I was thinking that His promise to be with me in hard times was one of sympathetic but helpless companionship. I would trudge through a deep and ever-deepening lake of problems and despair, barely keeping my head above the rising surface, while next to me little Jesus treaded water, hoping I would make it while He timidly stood by and wished it would all hurry up and be over.

I was wrong to think of God that way. Absolutely, God had the capability to fix it. God does have the power to do something and, in fact, He is doing something. He allowed Ted to go his own way, as is our son's prerogative. God allowed me to go through Ted's rebellion with him, in order that I might learn humility, trust and endurance. My prosaic suburban faith was being crudely fertilized by the crud of this experience. My character grew stronger, though, with every discipline, with every hard talk, every call to forgive and every decision to love.

Jesus promised us trouble: "In the world you will have tribulation, but take courage; I have overcome the world." John 16:33.

20

He who has the power to overcome the world could snap His fingers and change our son. But, for now, He chooses not to. Committed to that decision, He gets in the water with me. He chooses to be wet and cold and sore right next to me, feeding me words of encouragement, available to grab my arm with His strong hand when the current pulls my feet out from under me.

When our children were young, we took a road trip to South Dakota with some family friends. One of our friends' little boys was naughty so, as we gathered at the next rest stop for a cool ice cream cone, the little boy was denied what the rest of us enjoyed. His mother told him that, although she would love a cold treat, she would not have ice cream either. Even though it was in her power to remove the pain that she knew to be for his benefit, she didn't, but shared the pain with him instead.

The trouble we endure may not be for our discipline but, any time we suffer pain or distress, God jumps in it with us. He doesn't look nervously out the windshield like a helpless, white-knuckled passenger while dangerous black ice covers the road. He takes the wheel, if we let Him, and steers us through what He knows is coming. "Stay in the car," He says, "but let Me drive. I know what's ahead." Our Father goes with us – not like a timid puppy, but as a capable truck driver. I don't want this trouble in my life but, if I need to go through it, I want Him with me. I need to know He will use it for something good. I endure better when I know there is meaning. The strong Jesus is with me. I know that He has my back.

Thank You, Lord, that we endure nothing without You by our side. Thank You that, if I need to scale this mountain, You are my partner and rope. Everything I face in my life is with Your permission. Thank You for getting in the pain with me.

Lord, I pray that, if I have to do this, I will be the best mom I can be -- whatever that looks like. I don't want to fight against You. Instead, let me remember that You are for me.

Day 10. Alien Invasion

"Consider it all joy, my brethren, when you encounter various trials, knowing that the testing of your faith produces endurance. And let endurance have its perfect result, that you may be perfect and complete, lacking in nothing. But if any of you lacks wisdom, let him ask of God, who gives to all men generously and without reproach, and it will be given to him."

James 1:2-5

I told God matter-of-factly, "This mom thing used to be fun but now it's not. I didn't know raising teenagers would be like this. I feel as though my investment has not paid off. Also, a footnote: I don't like it. In fact, one might say I hate it." After an incident with Ted, I stomped down to the rec room and stated to my husband, "I'm going for a walk and when I get back I want to know where I go to resign." My husband looked at me calmly and said, "I don't think you can do that."

I used to see myself as an amusing and creative mom. After my boys passed age 12, however, the job description changed without my permission and I no longer felt qualified. One summer, without warning, no one wanted to go to the museum or my cousin's lake cottage. The bright days in which our children splashed in the city pool and twirled on tire swings had evolved into an overcast season of policing and concerns.

Against my will, I became a watch-dog, a punching bag, a bouncer who spent time thinking up creative discipline for sassy mouths and bad attitudes. I had regular bouts of discouragement and bewilderment. I wanted to be silly again, inventing some new adventure to do on a summer day, not dealing with the attitudes of party-poopers. Their sense of wonder seemed lost under a messy pile of moodiness. These were hard days for me for which I felt unprepared.

"Nothing stays the same," my mother says; but, as a young mom, I had no reason to think that my children would not. I believed that, if I filled their childhood with talk of Jesus and the sweet, lovely things of life, they would skip the adolescent transition time of angst and arrive gently on the shore of maturity. They put away childish things and brought out their pre-adult lives before I was ready.

So I educated myself on teenage behavior and asked questions of seasoned parents and youth pastors. I chose seminars on parenting teens and talked to other moms of my age and stage. I prayed for wisdom. Gradually, I began to understand my sons better, to lighten up and remember how I had acted as a teen. I learned that their character weaknesses can also be their strongest attributes and the reverse as well.

The book of James says that the testing of our faith produces endurance. "Let endurance have its perfect result that we may be perfect and complete, lacking in nothing."[5] Perfect and complete, lacking in nothing, sounds to me like something worth hanging in for. "Consider it all joy" is an appeal to take the blanket off my head and find an up side.

The opportunities young moms have at parks and play groups to compare notes on the stages of pre-schoolers have few counterparts for moms of teenagers. By the teenage years, we are often busy with jobs, intense volunteering and our kids' extra-curricular activities that take on lives of their own. We have no idea– at least I didn't – about what behavior is normal, what is not, and how to deal with either.

Do you agree that much of being the mother of a teenager is in the trial and error category? I absolutely think it is. I learned that, as idyllic as I had tried to make their childhood, they were not exempt from the adolescent rites of passage and choice-making. Never will I be a sage in all things teenage, but I have accumulated a long list of what-not-to-do's that I'm happy to share.

The point is that these years with our kids can be trying, but they are just as much an investment as were the sweet years when they were little. We built a foundation and an infrastructure back then. Now must come the reinforcement, insulation and finishing work. Persevere to end well in raising your son or daughter. Ask for wisdom. Find some joy. Renowned family expert James Dobson says of the teenage years, "Get through it and get them through it." Enjoy what God builds into your character while you carry on the construction.

Thank You, Lord, that there is nothing unusual about what I am experiencing. I may not have expected this kind of turmoil but, while I am in the middle of it, I appreciate Your promise to use it to make me more like Christ. Thank You also for the knowledge that this time won't last forever, so help me enjoy all that I can in the now.

Lord, I pray that I will not be a crabby, complaining mom fighting the development that must come in being a parent. I don't want disappointment or bitterness to characterize me. Would You help me to retain a sense of humor and an intentional concentration on the cares and needs of others? I want to be someone my children and others are happy to see.

Day 11.   Don't Just Do Something – Stand There

"Be still and know that I am God."

Psalm 46:10

Stand
Tell me what do you do when you've done all you
can,
and it seems like it's never enough?
Tell me what do you say, when your friends turn
away,
and you're all alone, so alone?
Tell me what do you give, when you've given your
all,
and it seems like you can't make it through?
You just stand, when there's nothing left to do.
You just stand, watch the Lord see you through.
Yes, after you've done all you can – you just stand.

After you've done all you can,
After you've prayed and cried, cried and prayed
All through the night,
After you plant your feet,
Squared your shoulders,
Hold your head up, and wait on Him.
He's gonna come through, yes He will.

After you've done all you can,
You just stand.[6]

We seem to always have plenty of things we can do to help our children. We can hire a tutor, practice with them in the backyard, discipline more or differently, introduce a hobby, sit with them while they do a difficult task or even give them schooling at home.

My husband and I had done everything we could think of to bring our son Ted out of his teenage tailspin. We had disciplined *ad nauseam*. We listened, talked, read books, gathered information from others, took him to counseling, prayed and fasted.

I remember the day I ran out of things I could do to help Ted. It was spring break and he was home from college for the week. We were going to paint our kitchen, go to an outlet mall, see some movies and check out the museum. He didn't want to do half of those things. He said he couldn't, that he didn't have it in him. He was silent, sullen, secretive and sad.

He watched television alone while I went to the kitchen and filled my brush with white paint and knelt in front of the cabinet door. Tears fell down my face, accompanied by silent deep sobs in my chest. There must be something I hadn't thought of, more that we could do. What do desperate people in this situation try next? Nothing came to mind. I felt physically sick and heart-heavy.

"God," I said, "I am going down. I will either crash and burn with Ted or I can cast this entirely on You. This sadness is so intense that, if I do not release it, I will be useless to everyone."

I realized that I could not live in that cave of grief and had to make a choice for myself. As I detached myself from the self-inflicted responsibility of doing one more thing which would help free Ted, I was able to get up and breathe. I stood.

Nothing had actually changed and I won't tell you that my cares were gone, but something was different. I felt lighter. I handed my backpack of rocks -- the heaviness of Ted's problems that I carried -- to God, and He took it. I could function. I could wait. I could keep going. "When my spirit grows faint within me, it is You who know my way."

Thank You, Lord, for taking on my load. Sometimes I give it to You and then I take it back. It seems there should always be something I can do to help my child. I know for sure that there is always something *You* can do. Show me how to let go and let You.

26

Lord, I pray for the ability to release my child to Your care. It seems irresponsible not to be orchestrating the next thing, but sometimes I have no idea what is the next thing. Teach me to wait on You. Teach me to rest in You.

Day 12. Hovercraft

"He found him a desert land, and in the howling waste of a wilderness; He encircled him, He cared for him, He guarded him as the pupil of His eye. Like an eagle that stirs up its nest, that hovers over its young, He spread His wings and caught them; He carried them on His pinions. The Lord alone guided him, and there was no foreign god with him.'"

Deuteronomy 32:11

This story, written by Moses about God's care for Jacob, gives us something we can pray for our children. I have certainly felt that Ted was in a figurative desert land, wandering in the howling waste of a wilderness. In this word-picture, God is encircling, caring, and protectively guarding His own as one would protect the pupil of one's eye. God hovers. He catches falling young ones and carries them on His wings.

Oh, that God would pluck our children out of the dangerous places they are in, fly them away to safety and drench them with affirming attention. Our dream is that "no foreign god would be with him" – not alcohol or other drugs, sex, a toxic boyfriend or girlfriend, food obsessions, bad friends or the allure of some deviant lifestyle.

Jill Briscoe gives a message about the hovering Spirit of God. She used to pray for her teenagers that the Spirit, who can go where mothers cannot go, would hover over them in school, at parties, in the car, and on dates. Hover, as defined by Webster, is "to remain suspended over a place or object." I love the thought that the Spirit can remain suspended over Ted as he goes out on the weekend, ambles through his school day, and interacts with girls, teachers and friends.

Although it is a tempting idea, chaining Ted to the patio furniture would not accomplish much in his character development. My husband often reminds me that our job as parents is not just to protect our children, but to guide them through the mistakes they make while under our roof in order to prepare them for the world without us. We want them to practice independence, not restrict them to the point of incapacity. I'd rather our son would learn from the mistakes I made at his age and skip his altogether. I wish I could superimpose on him the lessons I learned the hard way, but I can't.

Although it is impossible to learn by osmosis, there is something that God has given to us instead – His Spirit. The Holy Spirit teaches. He is my son's conscience. He protects and He hovers. He has power that I will never have. He goes where I can never go. He hovers, not smothers. He allows some bad choices and protects from others. I will never fully know how God has rescued me from dangers, but I know enough of them to trust that He can and does.

The saying "God can't be everywhere and so He made mothers" is so untrue. Mothers can't (and shouldn't) be everywhere, and so He sent His spirit. Not poetic enough for a plaque, but accurate.

As we release our children into the world each day, we function better knowing that, although they may trip and even fall, they are under the watchful eye of God, who tracks their every move and notices each heart rip and tear drip. Into His omnipotent, omniscient, powerful and tender care we can entrust our most precious, volatile hot potato. Hovering: better Him than me.

Thank You, Lord, that You have my child covered. I can trust You with him, knowing that You are right there, hovering. Thank you that, through Your design, my child gains independence from me and dependence on You.
Lord, I pray that Your Spirit will hover over my child -- today, tonight, this weekend. As he meets various friends in various places, hover over him. Be where I cannot be. Do what I cannot do and ultimately, God, show him the path to You.

Day 13. I Know Exactly How You Feel

"During the days of Jesus' life on earth, He offered up prayers and petitions with loud cries and tears to the one who could save Him from death and He was heard because of His reverent submission."
Hebrews 5:7

A friend sent the verse above to me in an email and said, "I had never really seen that before and now I wonder, what did Jesus care about so much that He prayed with loud cries and tears?"

I have been known to talk to God and to myself with loud cries and tears. Have you? Mine were over our son who refused to give in to a God who wanted so deeply to help him. Maybe Jesus was praying over the children He was desperate to care for, but who would have no part of it. Maybe He was praying that God would deliver Him from the complexities and ugliness of this world. I definitely have wished for that relief.

Like us, Jesus prayed with loud cries and tears. Like you, He felt sick with sadness over people he loved and the circumstances of His life. He may not have liked it, but he didn't fight it. God made it necessary for Him to go through dramatic suffering so that we have a savior who knows exactly how penetrating and intense human pain is. "I know how you feel. I've been there," He can truthfully say to us, with sympathy, empathy, knowledge and victory.

He was not immune to the exact heartbreak and hurt that we know. Many of his children rejected who He was and all that He taught them. They mocked and ridiculed Him, they spit on Him, they insulted Him, they hit Him, they ignored Him, they made fun of Him, they thought they knew more than Him, they flung obscene gestures at Him, they tried to intimidate Him. His hurt was as intense as yours has ever been.

Fortunately, Jesus is not a pathetic fatality. He was never a victim. Truth won out as He proved His God identity, not by force but by allowing God to play out His power in raising Him from the dead. He experienced agony as we do, but the resurrection cleared our path to God so that we can confidently ask for the mercy and grace we need in our most desperate times. As if that wasn't enough, He sent the Holy Spirit to give us more power than we could ever use up. The work is done. The gift has been given. The power is available.

There was a reason for it all. Can you believe that for yourself? Can you believe that all that you walk through with your child is not just a cruel torture to which you have been subjected by chance? I admit that I often don't care what good will result, I just want out. Getting out is not an option when you are equipped with all you need to stay and see it through.

Jesus doesn't send you down a path He has not traveled Himself. He was so real that He too asked God to save Him from the misery, but that was not the plan. He did what He had to do. When it was over, His obedience had changed everything. It was all new.

I have asked God to yank me out of this place, but I am still here. I have to do what I have to do and, when this time passes, I want to be an advertisement for an enduring obedience to God.

"When my spirit was overwhelmed within me, Thou didst know my path."[7]

Thank You, Lord, that my loud cries and tears are familiar to You. Thank You that, like Jesus, what I go through is not futile and has purpose. Thank You that this hard time in my life teaches me to go to You and to know You like I never have before.

Lord, I pray that You will show me how this very hard road I'm on might help someone else. Give me a message for someone else when I get into the light. Use my suffering and turn it into something good. One day, make all things new.

Day 14. When the Lights Go Out

In his famous devotional <u>My Utmost for His Highest</u>, Oswald Chambers wrote,

> At times God puts us through the discipline of darkness to teach us to heed Him. Song birds are taught to sing in the dark, and we are put into the shadow of God's hand until we learn to hear Him...
>
> Are you in the dark just now in your circumstances, or in your life with God?
>
> ...When you are in the dark, listen, and God will give you a very precious message for someone else when you get into the light.[8]

It is difficult to know exactly what is wrong when your child acts like a prodigal. We knew for sure that Ted was in a very dark place. I lived the truism that a mother is only as happy as her saddest child, and so Ted's dark place was my dark place.

I read and re-read these verses during those years: "If I say, 'Surely the darkness will overwhelm me, and the light around me will be night, even the darkness is not dark to You, and the night is as bright as the day. Darkness and light are alike to you.'" Psalm 139:11-12.

My darkness is not dark to God. He can see in it, and He knows where He is going. He knows where He is taking me in all of this. He knows how to get there. It is not the route I want to go, but I have this choice: I can bump into walls alone, or take His hand and let Him lead me through it.

The apostle Paul did not want to be shipwrecked, Peter the disciple did not relish spending time in jail and Joseph of the Old Testament would have liked to be anywhere but the pit where his brothers tossed him. Still, while in those dark places, they looked to God as their light.

Maybe you feel like you spend each waking hour in the dark. Did you know that this desperate time of your life has purpose? Bryan Loritts, teacher and pastor, has said that God is up-to-the-minute on where, how and why He allows difficult things in our lives. "I can trust you with this weight," God says to us, "I'm building something." I jotted this down on a small Post-It note and pull it out regularly. " ... *I'm building something*." I had no idea what God was doing. Even though I hated the process, I hoped what He was building in our son and in me would be worth this pain. May what He has built in the darkness, here in this house, be used as a light somewhere else.

Thank You, Lord, for understanding that we do not like darkness. It is the unknown. It is threatening and foreboding. Thank You that You are in there with us, speaking and guiding, hearing our cry and holding our hands. Thank You that You are using it for good. You are building something.

Lord, I pray that You will be very real to us in our darkness. Teach us to hear You speak just as You taught Peter, Paul and Joseph. We may not be able to see what is ahead of us, but we can listen to You along the way.

Day 15. Beware to Compare

"Behold, children are a gift of the Lord; The fruit of the womb is a reward. Like arrows in the hand of a warrior, So are the children of one's youth."

Psalm 127:3, 4

Our good friends were staying overnight in my son's room. I felt uneasy about the posters of certain musicians that hung on the walls in that room. I didn't love the posters when they went up but, in the context of those years, the battle was one not worth fighting. Our house embraces many different kinds of music, but no one was listening to contemporary Christian radio as I thought they should. Our friends' kids listened exclusively to Christian music and had sports posters on their bedroom walls. I told my husband that I really, really wished our guests did not have to lie in a bed that night staring at an avant-garde member of a popular band wearing a weird costume. It made me feel ashamed.

As we sat talking on our bed with the door closed, my husband looked intently at me and asked "Sarah, do you want different children?"

"No," I responded. "I want different posters." He replied: "Our children are who they are and these are their rooms. Until now, we have allowed them to put up certain posters. Why would we take them down today—because they are not the ones we think our friends would choose? I like who our boys are. I don't want anyone else's children. This is their taste right now."

I skulked away, only slightly consoled but generally convinced that I was majoring on a minor issue. My pride was the issue here, not the posters. Whether they were good or bad, they were not the image I wanted to portray to our friends. I was afraid they wouldn't approve, that they would think me less of a mother.

After our friends went back home I thought, "Why do I assume people expect me or my family to be something other than what we are? Why do I assume our dear friends would sit in judgment of me or

34

my kids whom they practically love as their own? They don't and they didn't. I wanted my children's tastes to comply with a model that would impress. I had my own criteria for what they should like and not like, and they were not buying it. They insisted on being themselves – frustrating!

On a walk, I was complaining to God that many of my friends -- it seemed like all of them -- had ultra-achieving children who raked in accomplishments, awards, starring roles and recognition like fallen leaves in a tree-filled yard. I placed exaggerated value in these things and they seemed constantly in my face. My children's résumés were sparse by comparison, and comparison is what got me in trouble.

On that same walk, I heard God sternly interrupt me as clearly as if He were behind me: "Enough of this. I gave you three children who are remarkable individuals. I have gifted them as much as anyone else, just differently. You know this, but you have turned this into some sort of contest that is all about you. You need to ask for and practice a thankful attitude and start concentrating on all that your children *are*, not what they don't do." Only one other time in my life have I sensed God's message to me so directly.

That started me working hard on my gratitude attitude. I resolved that, in every difficult situation, I would find two things for which to be thankful. In various future issues with our boys, I zeroed in on two "thank You God" things as my practice. It was remarkable what a difference this made. I became free to see the good in our children, and their unique sets of talents and strengths. I gained better perspective in the hard circumstances of raising them. I believed in them more. I think I loved them better.

Ironically, my sons have added significantly to their interests and accomplishments since that time, but that is not what I love about them. I'm so glad I realized that they are valuable not for what they do, but for who they are. I am proud of them for a kind word spoken, a good decision made, or some self-sacrifice, no matter how small, no matter who sees it or does not. There is so much to be thankful for in these gifts which are our children. Can we, can I, amplify the good in them enough to dwarf the foolish monster of pride we feed in ourselves?

"It is a wise man who does not grieve for the things which he has not, but rejoices for those which he has." Epicetus (c.50-120)

35

My children are a gift, and I don't want any other than the ones I was given. If I can practice thankfulness, I will appreciate the people with whom I am blessed.

Thank You, Lord, for the children You gave to me. I want to treat them and hold them like the gifts they are, not obsess about their accomplishments. Thank You for all that is exceptional about them. Let me embrace that and be thankful.

Lord, I pray that I would respect who my children are and not let my pride communicate to them that I wish they were someone else for the sake of my image. You have fashioned their distinct talents and gifts in concordance with what the world needs. They are made in Your image to point people to You, not to me.

Day 16. Who's in Charge Here?

"But Moses said to the people, 'Do not fear! Stand by and see the salvation of the Lord which He will accomplish for you today; for the Egyptians whom you have seen today, you will never see them again forever. 'The Lord will fight for you while you keep silent.'"

Exodus 14:13, 14

These words are from Moses just before God parted the Red Sea for the Israelites when they were trapped by their enemies, without a plan and utterly crazy with fear. I can relate to feeling cornered, helpless and beside myself when I don't see one single option of what to do next.

Do you see absolutely no way out of your child's circumstances without the insertion of a miracle? Stand by and see what God accomplishes while you keep silent. He will fight for you. I just can't love God enough for this passage. He almost says to me, "You don't have to think up something magical to say to your son that will change everything. You don't have to be sick with anticipation of another fight. I know there is nothing you have left in you right now, but I am asking you to do one thing -- stand and believe. Can you do that much?"

One of the more emotional days of trouble with Ted began with a phone call from the mom of one of his friends. She was alarmed by recent signs of descent she saw in her own son. As she talked, my breath shortened and I felt this deep sense of grief and responsibility – that the heartache was spreading like a contagious disease, and Ted was the carrier.

After that call, I had an appointment to get my van tire repaired. At the tire store, I stood waiting by the full length window, leaning on a pillar and unashamedly sobbing my way through a wad of tissues as I pretended to look out on passing traffic. "Well, God," I thought, "I am reduced to a dismal puddle in an auto shop, not caring who sees me or what they think. All that is within me seems to be draining out of my eyes and onto this dirty floor."

No less distraught later that afternoon, I drove my youngest son to his piano lesson. For that hour I stayed in the parked car and continued to cry out my discouragement. I stared out the windshield and pressed the repeat button on my van's CD player, listening as though the words to one song were all I had in the world. Steven Curtis Chapman's lyrics enabled me to picture a resolved Jesus, inches away from my face and firmly holding one of my shoulders in each large hand, looking me straight in the eyes and saying:

> I am the One who waved my hand and split the ocean.
> I am the One who spoke the words and raised the dead.
> And I've loved you long before I set the world in motion.
> I know all the fears you're feeling now, but do you remember who I am?[9]

God is capable of altering what is threatening and unchanging by a word from His lips, one word, at any time. That knowledge has kept me going when I see no indication that anything is even slightly turning in the right direction.

God knows every one of the fears I have right now. He knows that I'm afraid that our son will never choose to walk with Him, that Ted's choices will end badly, that he will take others down with him and that my heartache in seeing him throw so much away will never end. He knows the fears that I don't have the courage to whisper.

Can I remember who God is even in a state of dread and grief? Can I remember that He has never, ever abandoned me? Can I remember that God is today the same God who has done so much for me in the past? Can you?

Have you had a day like mine, a time of internal panic so acute you think you'll implode? Jesus has you firmly by the shoulders. Look Him in the eye as He looks inside you. Be quiet and let Him talk you down. Say His name. Remember who He is.

Thank You, Lord, that You are for me. Thank You that You understand how completely exhausted and afraid I am. Thank You that You have power and authority over everyone and everything. Thank

You that I can know that the things You say to me are absolutely true, and that this time of ordeal is not wasted time. You promise it isn't. **Lord, I pray** that You will gently but firmly hold me by the shoulders and quiet me down. I can stand and believe if You will do the rest. I do pray that all this heartache will bring glory to You somehow and that You will use it for good. Help me to remember who You are.

Day 17. The Weak Link

"Above all, keep fervent in your love for one another, because love covers a multitude of sins."

I Peter 4:8

Tom is my dear friend, a widower with three boys, one of whom is significantly out of control. He called me on a certain night, sobbing: "I'm done Sarah. I've given up on him. I don't know what else to do. Nothing works. I'm ready to hand him over, turn him loose to the street and say, 'go figure it out yourself.'" Then he was silent, collecting himself enough to say "I've made many mistakes but I've tried everything I can think of. There's nothing left to do." Then he cried again.

Finally, I said softly, "You have not given up on him, Tom. You wouldn't be calling me now if you had given up on him."

Tom and I have both cried about our two lost boys, who are best friends with one another and chose similar paths of behavior. We have counseled, commiserated and provided comic relief to one another for years. Tom's wife died during the boys' 8th grade year. Tom had been a somewhat distant father, but took over immediately at his wife's passing. He drenched his three boys in love and attention. He began to cook, fill out health forms, attend school conferences, call teachers, do laundry and order dance corsages. He changed jobs so he could travel less and work out of his home. He battled his own personal demons while he monitored where his kids went, with whom and when they would return. He hosted his son's parties and began friendships with his friends.

Often, as his son rode in the back seat of my car checking in by cell phone, I would hear him say "I love you too, Dad" before they disconnected. Tom talked and listened, questioned and hugged. Tom juggled everything else so that he could handle the many crises with this son that peppered the years following the death of his wife. He never gave up. Maybe he made some mistakes -- I assured him we all do -- but what he did do was love, love, love, love. Sometimes, his love was in discipline, anger and honest exasperation. He did everything he could think of to do, and then he just loved.

Tom is one of my heroes. In the chaos and devastation of a family catastrophe, he rolled up his sleeves and became the father he said he should have been earlier. His son may have some emotional stones, even rocks in his path, but one thing he knows for sure -- he is loved. It's never too late for love.

When Ted was entering his senior year of high school, his last stretch at home before college, my husband and I talked in our bedroom one Sunday morning. We reflected on the realization that the two of us were facing the end of our daily parenting of Ted. Outside his open closet door, my husband draped his tie on a hook and then took me by the shoulders. He said: "Sarah, you have just one year left with Ted at home. Make it count. Love him, touch him, hug him, kiss him. I know you two have your issues with each other, but the most important thing you can do this year is to make sure he leaves here knowing you love him."

My husband was right and I tried to do that. In recent years, most of the exchanges with my son – sadly they were seldom conversations – had been primarily about behavior. I'm quite sure many were motivated by my fears, well-founded or not. In his senior year, I tried to take my fears to God and step up my show of love and encouragement to Ted. I asked God to show me more and more what I could celebrate about him and with him. This required a deliberate, conscious effort.

Toward the end of the summer, Ted and I sat on bleachers at a concert, listening to James Taylor among family and friends. I was struck by the simple wisdom in a song we heard: "Shower the people you love with love. Show them the way that you feel. You know, things are gonna be much better if you only will."[10]

Of course I loved my child. I was just weary in the work of being his parent. I had forgotten the single most important message to give him. I tried harder.

Thank You, Lord, that You make available more love to us than we can possibly pass on. You are happy to give us as much as we need.

Thank You for showing me that, no matter what I do or don't do for my child, the best thing I can do is to love him.

Lord, I pray that You will fill me with the courage and creativity to express love to my child. In the tension, the anger and the disappointment, let me show him that I love him fully, without regard for his behavior, just as You do for me.

Day 18. Who Can I Blame?

"And he said, 'Naked I came from my mother's womb, and naked I shall return there. The Lord gave and the Lord has taken away. Blessed be the name of the Lord.' Through all this Job did not sin nor did he blame God."

Job 1:20-22

"And he (Job) took a potsherd to scrape himself while he was sitting among the ashes. Then his wife said to him, 'Do you still hold fast your integrity? Curse God and die!' But he said to her, 'You speak as one of the foolish women speaks. Shall we indeed accept good from God and not accept adversity?'"

Job 2:8-10

After five years of her own situational heartache, a friend said to me in frustration, "I have been obedient to God. I have done everything I think He wants me to do, so why doesn't God fix it?" That, I concurred, is a very good question. Issues were mounting in our home while Ted was getting deeper into trouble. I was taking a walk one night when I tearfully, and with some anger, asked God out loud, "What else do You want from me? I am doing the best I can!" Later, I realized that God was not punishing me through the actions of our son. We had a problem, but God's motivation in allowing it to unfold was not mean or punitive.

Job was a blameless and upright man. God allowed Satan to test him, to bring heartache and hardship into his life to exhibit his loyalty to and trust in God. Why? I don't know all God's purposes in Job's life and I don't know all of them in mine. But I do know that God works out of love, wisdom, justice and goodness. If that is true of God, then what happens in my life, by circumstance or through the actions of people, is not to harm me but will be used for good. It doesn't feel good, but it is applied as a means to an end.

Certainly, this is tough to believe when a new day is worse than the one before or as Ruth Bell Graham says in her book about prodigals, "you wake up not from a nightmare, but to one."[11]

Regardless of my circumstances, I must admit that God remains unchanged from who He was in the past and who He says He is. He is not out to get me, quite the opposite, but He does carry out things His own way and He will not be coerced or bullied into adapting to my timetable.

I tend to forget the thousands, perhaps millions of blessings I have enjoyed in my life, just as I am tempted to call God out as unfair. I happily accepted the goodness of God in the sweet days when life was simpler and cares were few. Today, there are problems and I need Him more than ever. It is not my position to assess fault. God remains the same, and His love for me has not fluctuated. In the knowledge of that truth, I can say blessed is the name of the Lord.

Thank You, Lord, for what You are doing which I cannot see, in me and those I love. I trust in Your goodness even when I struggle to see it. Regardless of how I feel now, I am thankful for the blessings in my past and in my life today.

Lord, I pray for endurance during this season of pain and suffering. You have been kind and faithful to me in the past, and I hold fast to that memory as I walk through this season in my life. You will be faithful again.

Day 19. He Knows

"Be anxious for nothing, but in everything by prayer and supplication with thanksgiving let your requests be made known to God. And the peace of God, which surpasses all comprehension, shall guard your hearts and minds in Christ Jesus."

Philippians 4:6, 7

The following is taken from a journal entry in April of 2005:

"My grace is sufficient for you. Grace is the way I love you even though you don't do anything to earn it. I just do." I write to God, "My life is going by quickly Lord -- very quickly. Have I done, so far, what You wanted me to do? More importantly, am I, so far, what you want me to be?

For the first time this year I am aware of how You love me. You delight in me. You are crazy about me. Maybe You laugh at me and with me. Maybe You hit Your sides and laugh loudly when I do. Maybe You cry with me when I am sad.

After I discover drugs in Ted's backpack today, I drive 20 minutes downtown to the lakefront beach to cry and pray. I feel as though you are sitting right next to me on the park bench with both Your arms around me as I curl up into a ball of a person and weep.

Your head is next to mine and I almost hear You whisper to me, 'I know Darling. I know. Believe it or not, I know how much you want your Teddy to love Me. I know that you are desperate for him to turn His life over to Me. I know you are afraid. I completely understand that you feel rejected by him. So do I. The difference is that I can do something about it. Can you wait? Can You? I have stored up your prayers, tears, moanings and groanings for Teddy like jewels in a vault. One day when it's the right time I will unlock the vault and give back all of the treasures to you in the form of a Teddy who is all about Me. But you need to let Me pick the time. Wait for Me.

Just like you never forget where your children are, I never lose track of Teddy. I am always thinking of him, always working on him. I am moving things around in his life so that he will need Me so much he can't resist Me.'"

I note to myself the things I needed to turn over to God that day. Number six is "my anxieties." I write out 1 Peter 5: 6 & 7. "Humble yourselves, therefore, under the mighty hand of God, that He may exalt you at the proper time, casting all your anxiety upon Him, because He cares for you." "First," I wrote "humble myself enough to realize that I can't handle all this without His help."

Thank You, Lord, that Your grace is sufficient for me. Without a solution or a conclusion, Your grace is enough for me this hour and day.

Lord, I pray that I live out the time You have given me in a close relationship with You. In order to hear You, I must listen. In order to be comforted, I must let You in. In order to exchange my anxiety for peace, I need to tell You about it. In order to trust You, I need to know You and believe You are God.

Day 20. Expectations

"Train up a child in the way he should go. Even when he is old he will not depart from it."

Proverbs 22:6

What did you expect before you had your children? Did you expect, as I did, that if you read lots of books to them and took them to the library that they would grow up to be readers? Did you expect that, if you fed your baby vegetables and nothing sweeter than Cheerios, he or she would, as a result, be a healthy eater? Did you expect that, if you made cookies together for a sick neighbor, that one day your teen would say, "I think I'll go over and mow old Mrs. Clark's lawn today for free"? Did you expect that, if you read nightly Bible stories and said sweet prayers at bedtime, your children would inexorably move into having their own deep devotions every morning before middle school?

I am not sure where I got those false assurances, although I have sometimes been quick to blame some person or organization for promising them to me. I think it has more to do with my starry-eyed naiveté than with a rock-solid guarantee that I thought I had heard somewhere. So often, I talk to moms who are disappointed that everything they have poured into their children seems to have seeped out their toes with nothing retained. The table manners, the thoughtfulness toward others, the dependence on God and His Word, the practice of prayer – "where did all those lessons go?" we ask, when we see our teens completely self-absorbed, leading undisciplined or chaotic lives. I thought if I taught and modeled certain traits, that I would have little-boy versions of Sarah at her best and not her worst. I did not realize, as my husband reminds me, that "they are not you." And, oh yes, they are not finished products either.

I heard a child psychologist say in an interview, when asked about parents' expectations for children, that "childhood is all about learning. It's the forum we have for making mistakes and correcting ourselves.

It's the process we go through to become functioning adults. It's the path, not the end." Pretty simple thought, but profound nonetheless.

We train up a child in the way he or she should go – or we try to. "In the way he should go," by the way, is footnoted as "according to his way." The cross reference is Ephesians 6:4: "And, fathers, do not provoke your children to anger; but bring them up in the discipline and instruction of the Lord." Proverbs says that "Even when he is old he will not depart from it." At what age is "old?" Is it 14 or 18 or 21? Is it 40 or 60 or 80?

We are not told her exact age, but I do know that Jesus' mother Mary was never described as old and in fact was probably a young teenager when she had Jesus. Daniel in the Old Testament was in his teens when he was taken to Babylon. He was called a youth. David was "a youth" when he slew Goliath. I think maybe God does not think of teenagers as old. This thought came to me when I was working in my yard one day, feeling that a lot of what I had taught my son had not taken root. "Lord, Proverbs says that when he is old he will not depart from his training. Oh, he's not really old yet, is he?"

I cannot find a Biblical promise about being a book-reader or a healthy eater. As sinful creatures with their own wills, there are no guarantees about what choices our children will make as they grow up. But, to a point, we can be patient with our children and recall what we were doing and thinking when we were their age. Maybe you were astute and mature, but most of us were still making mistakes, with very little wisdom and totally in the dark about most things rational. In recent years research has shown that the section of the adolescent brain associated with consequences, decision-making and danger-risk is not fully developed until approximately age 25.

I asked world-renowned Christian speaker and author Jill Briscoe, "What would you have done differently when your children were teenagers?" "I wouldn't have worried so much," she said. Although I did not get a follow-up question with Jill, I have to wonder if she said that because, when you see your children reach adulthood, many parental fears are proven unfounded. Our expectations are often just unrealistic. They often are not based on promises. What we are to do is just to train the child in the way he or she should go, and we leave the results to God. So many moms realize, during the teen years, there is no other choice but to trust God with all we have taught and modeled so far. We just do not have the same control over the outcome as we had expected to have.

Thank You, Lord, that our only expectations should be that You are faithful and true. We can expect what You promise, but we cannot expect what we dream up on our own. Thank You that You have a design for my child, that he is not me and that You have made him according to Your own plan and purpose. Thank You for who my child is.

Lord, I pray that You would help me train my child as best I can in the instruction and discipline of You, and then trust that You will work it out in him or her. Let me relax in the knowledge that I don't have to worry, You are in control.

Day 21. Never Give Up

"Love is patient, love is kind, and is not jealous; love does not brag and is not arrogant, does not act unbecomingly; it does not seek its own, is not provoked, does not take into account a wrong suffered, does not rejoice in unrighteousness, but rejoices with the truth; bears all things, believes all things, hopes all things, endures all things. Love never fails..."

I Corinthians 13:4-8a

The other night, I watched a Batman movie with my husband. At various times, a young Bruce Wayne says to his butler and guardian Alfred, "You still aren't giving up on me, are you, Alfred?" In his stately British accent, with a sparkle in the eye and a slight smile, Alfred replies, "Never."

No one needs to convince us to love our children. Part of our heartache in the bad choices they make is that we love them so desperately, so completely, that it is painful to see them walk a path which we know will bring certain calamity into their lives. As the bad choices escalate, continue or repeat themselves, we grow weary and lose hope. In the latter of many years of struggle with Ted, I became unhappy with my preoccupation with him and his deeds. With his issues always churning in my head and tugging on my heart, I longed for a different state of mind, another focus of my prayers and a moving on of sorts. To lovingly detach – if that is possible with a child – can be necessary and wise, but it's another thing to declare someone hopeless.

Love doesn't give up. Love gives over, but not up. More than once I told God, "I need to be done with this. I don't want to do this anymore. Get me out of this mothering role. It is too much for me." But then I would pull out His definition of love and realize that there is no quitting. Love is patient. It bears all things, believes all things, hopes all things, endures all things. Love doesn't fail. Love doesn't give up on someone. I can give our son over to God but I don't need to give up on him.

I began to think about how God doesn't give up on me when I am stuck in a virtual ditch, spinning my wheels frantically and grinding myself deeper and deeper into mud. He figuratively stands in front of me and waves me forward with His hands, slowly guiding me out, even if it means backing up first. I want to do that for Ted. I want to be waiting for him when he is ready to come out of the ditch he is in. I want to be patient with him as God is patient with me. I want to bear, to believe, to hope, to endure and to never fail him. I need God's help, because although I greatly love him, the hard season is exhausting and I want it to be over.

I think of my friend Jen, whose only child rebelled against her for years with cruel words and disobedient behavior. In my judgmental attitude, I thought I knew what Jen should do to react to her daughter. But now, 10 years later, Jen's daughter has come to embrace Jesus Christ as her Savior and is grateful to her mom for all she endured during her angry years of rebellion. Her mom was waiting for her to come back. Her love was patient.

Tough love can be appropriate. It is important to establish boundaries with children who manipulate. We then look to God's wise counsel and expert opinion, and not to a rule or someone else's action as our benchmark for how we handle a difficult teen. In whatever form it takes, they need to know we have never given up on the person they are inside. How would I feel if God gave up on me? In His persistent love, He never does. That keeps me going.

Thank You, Lord, that You bother to define love for me. Love is not just mushy warm feelings but a code of conduct to which I hold myself. Thank You for the encouragement of knowing that love never fails. I can't go wrong loving my children, even if they don't deserve it or receive it.

Lord, I pray that I would be found faithful to stay the course and live love to my child. When I feel inside like giving up, show me something, bring to mind something that persuades me to persevere. Remind me that You never give up on either me or my child. Help me to bear, believe, hope and endure all things.

Day 22. Try to Stump Him

"Is anything too difficult for the Lord?"

Genesis 18:14

God asked Abraham this question after He told Abraham that he and his elderly wife would have a son in their old age. Sarah laughed. Two seniors who had been unable to have children during normal child-bearing years were now about to have a baby when their friends were welcoming great-grandchildren. I am sure they had resigned themselves to being childless long before, although they no doubt still carried the heartache. What they heard might have sounded absurd to them, but to God it was just His plan being carried out how and when He wanted.

Have you thought your child to be too difficult for the Lord? You hear other mothers talk about their frustrations with their children's behavior and you think, "Give me an hour and I will tell you about some *real* problems." You might listen to prayer requests about the infractions or struggles of other teens and decide to not even open your mouth about yours because they are so much more in quantity and severity. Many times, you could volunteer something that would probably shock them but you hold back because it would make people uncomfortable.

In a quiet time, you pause and think about the latest thing you need to deal with in your teen's life, and all of a sudden you are stacking their recent actions on top of each other like cardboard boxes that get bigger as they get higher. How many more can go on the pile until they crash to the ground? When will it happen? How will it happen? This is when we could decide that it is all simply too much for God to handle.

Our teen surpassed minor violations a long time ago, and now has moved into the land-of-no-return. There were years when the problems with Ted would consistently go from bad to worse, and then worse still. I struggled to believe that God was not in over His head. I reminded myself of the personal experience I have had with God, and the truth I know about Him and His Word. I would throw back on Him His promises that I see on my Bible page. He would never leave me. He was not wringing His hands. He was involved in Ted's life, whether I could see it or not. He was in control. He loves Ted beyond measure. He died for my son and was not about to disengage Himself from his life when things got hard.

He made the world and all that is in it, but could He handle this bucking young colt who seemed ready to break the ropes that held him? I would hang onto my faith like a child holds on to the remaining small corner of her baby blanket, rubbing it over and over to find some shred of security in her world.

"Is there anything too hard for the Lord? Is there anything too hard for Him? He is God the mighty One, He speaks the word and it gets done, is there anything too hard for the Lord?"[12] I listened to this song on my walks and held back the temptation to say, "Actually, there is something too hard for the Lord, and his name is..." The truth came to me that God can speak one word and change everything – a thought, an understanding, a perception, a condition. He can. I have seen Him do it in me.

> "So you're facing a trying situation, and you're trying hard to trust the One who's never failed you yet. Though you're trying hard to trust Him soon that faith has turned to fear, and just before you give it up, He'll hold your heart, lift it up, and the answer comes to you loud and clear -- in the form of the answer that you hear, "is there anything too hard for the Lord?"[13]

If God were to share the future with us as He did with Abraham and Sarah, maybe we would scoff with a "yeah, right," or perhaps we would be able to respond, "Okay. Nothing is too difficult for You."

Thank You, Lord, that I have the opportunity to trust You to work in a very difficult situation. Thank You that Your promises are true and that everything I know about Your faithfulness in my life is very real. Thank You that nothing, and no one, is too difficult for You.

Lord, I pray that You would give me the faith to hand this heartache over to You and believe that You know what to do with it. Give me the faith to wait, even a very long time, as Abraham and Sarah did; in the meantime, let me be found faithful to You in this place.

Day 23. Desert Walking

"They wandered in the wilderness in a desert region; they did not
find a way to an inhabited city. They were hungry and thirsty;
their soul fainted within them. Then they cried out to the Lord in
their trouble; He delivered them out of their distresses, He led
them also by a straight way, to go to an inhabited city. Let them
give thanks to the Lord for His lovingkindness and for His wonders
to the sons of men! For He has satisfied the thirsty soul, and the
hungry soul He has filled with what is good."

Psalm 107:4-9

This week my friend has come to visit me from Texas. She is ten
years younger than me and considers me to be one of her three favorite
mentoring moms. When her husband was in medical school here, two
of my friends and I took Tracy under our wing. We tried to help and
encourage her through the trying years of starting a family with a
totally preoccupied husband. It has been over five years since she
moved, and three since her last visit.

I don't remember anything about her last visit. She didn't stay with
me and we might have only grabbed a coffee. All three of us
mentoring moms were in crisis mode: one of us had a child with a
serious eating disorder, one had a child in the throws of deep
depression and I was on watch with my son in rebellion. Tracy did not
know the extent of our children's problems; we didn't even take the
time to fill her in.

Now she is back again and there is much chatter about her five young
children, church programs, friends and community activities. She asks
me questions to catch up on the last several years. I don't have nearly
the volume of information to report that she does, and certainly not the
plethora of participation in events and tasks. I decide this morning that
I am coming off to her as a boring drop-out. I suspect that she might
leave feeling disappointed in me that I have not branched out or grown
in my interests. As I clear the breakfast dishes, I tell her the reason.
For five years, God has given me only one major assignment – our

middle son. He has used me in other ways, but mostly I have stayed within the ring of fire surrounding Ted. It has been an all-consuming time.

I did not want it to be all-consuming. In addition to a part-time job, I was a full-time on-call mom to three boys, one who was extremely high-maintenance. I sought to distract myself with a leadership position, but found that the responsibilities were an addition to my pile, not a distraction from it. I made myself suddenly responsible for managing 12 strangers in a new small group when the surplus of people in my personal life were already wanting for attention My other part-time job was to fine-tune my prayer life in which I participated all day, every day. That was my reality. Not glamorous, not public, not fun, but where God had me, of that I was sure.

The past years have been a wandering in the desert of sorts. The journey has been uncomfortable and exhausting; most times, there has been only a mirage of hope on the horizon suggesting that I was getting any closer to a place of relief. I walked it without finding a way to an inhabited city, no place where I could find camaraderie with other parents wandering in the same sort of desert.

I sat on my bed explaining in tears to Tracy that I don't want her to be disappointed in me. Walking next to a child through rebellion is not a place of prestige, respect or accomplishment. In a lot of ways, it is just sort of being there, being available to deal with what happens next. It is humbling and lonely. "Everything else was on hold," I explained to her.

Tracy's eyes filled up and she quietly said, "I'm sorry. I didn't know."

Receiving her sweet empathy almost caught me off guard. Having a child revolt against you is indeed like a death, the death of the happy, carefree little person you once knew. Surprisingly I then found myself rebounding with anxiousness to tell Tracy of the good that has come of it. I told her the situation; now she needed to know how God was all over it.

I became so close with my Father in Heaven, I told her, so close to Jesus. He became my friend, my confidante, my listener, my counselor, my comforter. I learned how to pray on a whole other level I had never known before. I sought out information and counsel that benefited me. I learned to ask God for truth, no matter how hard it was to confront. I learned that, even when I am in a dry and monochromatic place, God goes to great lengths to show love to me in ways I don't expect. Even though I would get up each day and still find myself stuck in this desert time of parenting, He would be waiting for me, to talk and tell me things through His Word. He would do things, mostly small kind things, that were like gift bouquets of lush color or a refreshing breeze blowing over me, if only for a moment. There were times when I felt like He held an umbrella of shade over me long enough so that I could cool off and keep walking. I would yell for Him and He would be there with a remedy as a canteen of water. So often, I would hear Him say to my heart "Sarah, you have to walk through this desert. Sometimes you even have to crawl. I know you hate it, but I am here and I will not, for an instant, ever leave your side."

A wise mother I know, who went through a long, hard place with her daughter as a teenager, told me "I would not ever wish something like that to happen to anyone else. Yet I would not trade the things I learned and how close I got to God for anything in the world."

Thank You, Lord, that You are at work, even in the desert. Thank You that where I am, You are. Thank You that, no matter how bad things get, You find ways to show me Your lovingkindness – even in the small things. I feel You near me.
Lord, I pray that You will give me endurance. Keep me true to my calling as a mom, no matter how exhausting and discouraging this time becomes. You were exhausted and discouraged with Your children too, Lord. Help me go the distance as You did and find joy in You and You alone.

Day 24. New Every Morning

"How blessed is he whose help is the God of Jacob, whose hope is in the Lord his God; who made heaven and earth, the sea and all that is in them; who keeps faith forever; who executes justice for the oppressed; who gives food to the hungry. The Lord sets the prisoners free."

Psalm 146:5

The grayness of this morning and the temperature drop of the forecast make me tearful as I think of other mothers like me who are starting their days with grayness in their hearts. "What will this day bring to me?" and "what unwelcome surprises await me?" they wonder. Through the long winter of Ted's dark place, I longed for warmth, sunlight and small events to distract me from the sadness which had become part of my condition.

As I look back on those years, the feelings I had still so much a part of me, I think of the consistency of God. I never had to wonder, when I got up, what He would be like, what wild card of His temperament He would deal to me, what scary or unsettling thing He would say to me. There were no eggshells to walk on when I went to meet with Him in the morning, only the solid ground of what He has always been. I didn't have to sense a mood with God or anticipate a tense situation when I announced something to Him. I am thankful that God is not a volatile complexity of emotional reactions. He never changes. His love for me is the same immeasurable expanse it was yesterday, and will be tomorrow. I can't see a corner of it is ever missing, and no one can take it from me.

He had a fresh kindness delivered to me daily. I could almost see His desperate desire to encourage me. A friend would deliver a premature birthday present to me, knowing I needed it now. My husband would cradle me in his arms or our oldest son would recount something very, very funny about his day. My youngest son would discuss at dinner, a current issue about which he felt strongly. One hard day, I found a years-old dirty orange sticky note in the back of my desk drawer that was penciled, "Mom, I love you a lot," written by the Ted when he was little, who had recently professed to hate me. I might open an unexpected email from a friend, hear a new sweet song on the radio, or trade wits with a delightful store clerk.

One difficult day after a bad happening with Ted, I spent my half hour on the health club elliptical machine in silent sobs. I had never met the trainer who noticed, and came over to ask me gently, "what's wrong?" When I briefly explained, he told me that his strong mother had helped him out of a very bad time in his teenage life, and he offered me some thoughts from his own experience. I regrouped, my spirits were lifted and I left the club encouraged. God was careful to take care of me even if He wasn't taking the hurdle away.

As we sang a song about God's faithfulness in church last Sunday, I wanted to sing it to Ted's goateed face. I wanted him to know that, no matter what he presented to me each day of those years, God had been faithful. His consistent love never changed toward Ted or me. Every day, God thought up new mercies for me, whether it was at the health club, the chatty greeting of a friend or reassuring words from my mother. I can only imagine the mercies God showed to Ted himself. So many bad things that could easily have happened did not. The things that did happen came with their own set of mercies to get us through the day. There will be more tomorrow.

> The Lord's lovingkindnesses indeed never cease,
> For His compassions never fail.
> They are new every morning;
> Great is Thy faithfulness.[14]

Thank You, Lord, for not changing. Thank You for waking me up each morning with mercies that You think up especially for me. Thank You that You know what I need and You know how to meet my need perfectly. Thank you that I do not hesitate to say that You are faithful. You always have been. You always will be.

Lord, I pray that You would bring back my child. I pray that one day he would recognize Your faithfulness for him and gratefully tell others.

Day 25. The Great Escape

"Fear and trembling come upon me; and horror has overwhelmed me. And I said, 'O that I had wings like a dove! I would fly away and be at rest. Behold I would wander far away, I would lodge in the wilderness. I would hasten to my place of refuge from the stormy wind and tempest."

Psalm 55:5-8

"He who dwells in the shelter of the Most High will abide in the shadow of the Almighty. I will say to the Lord, 'My refuge and my fortress, My God, in whom I trust!' For it is He who delivers you from the snare of the trapper, and from the deadly pestilence. He will cover you with His pinions, and under His wings you may seek refuge; His faithfulness is a shield and bulwark. You will not be afraid of the terror by night, or of the arrow that flies by day."

Psalm 91:1-5

"Be gracious to me, O God, be gracious to me, for my soul takes refuge in Thee; and in the shadow of Thy wings I will take refuge, Until destruction passes by."

Psalm 57:1

God understands that sometimes we want to escape. Certainly, David wanted an out when the heat was turned up in his life. Jesus left crowds to be alone with God. As His sphere of influence expanded, it must have been a challenge to find an isolated spot. I imagine there were times when the only retreat was in His head, with the Father.

A new trouble can make me feel as though I am in rising water moving up from my knees to my stomach to above my nose, so that I cannot breathe. I have often wanted to escape my life, to get in my car and keep driving, to hole up in a hotel room somewhere and just sleep for days. Sometimes I want to run away to just about anywhere but here.

There is a place to go and a person to see who is always available, always open, always listening, always quiet, always counseling, always safe, always confidential, always satisfying. God is a refuge. He is a place to hide. He invites us to sneak away, walk away or even run away to Him. He *is* security and protection.

After a tough truth had been revealed or a gut-wrenching confrontation occurred, I go into my dark bedroom and lie face down, diagonally on my bed, to find that secret place with God and try to assess what just happened. He quiets me down. Sometimes I drive to a lonely place, or even a very public location and sit in my car or on a park bench and invite Jesus to come with me and together we would just be. At times, I stand face-to-face in a confrontation with my angry son and silently ask God in my head, "What should I do? What should I say? Help me, help me, help me."

Sometimes I tell my husband that I have to steal away for an hour because "I'm peopled out." The complexities of life leave me with the need to find breathing room for time in the presence of God.

No one can take away that place I find with God. Christ and me, whether we are alone and still or I talk and He listens. It is a safe place to be.

Thank You, Lord, for living in my heart so that I have constant access to You. Thank You for knowing my every thought, hurt and concern without a word from my lips. Thank You for being the great listener.
Lord, I pray that I would run, not walk, to my meeting place with You. Whether it is a room, a chair or behind my closed eyes, I want to be where You are.

Day 26. Larger than Life

"My voice rises to God, and I will cry aloud; my voice rises to God, and He will hear me. In the day of my trouble I sought the Lord; In the night my hand was stretched out without weariness; my soul refused to be comforted. When I remember God, then I am disturbed; when I sigh, then my spirit grows faint. Thou hast held my eyelids open; I am so troubled that I cannot speak. I have considered the days of old, the years of long ago. I will remember my song in the night; I will meditate with my heart; and my spirit ponders.

"Will the Lord reject forever: And will He never be favorable again? Has His lovingkindness ceased forever: Has His promise come to an end forever? Has God forgotten to be gracious? Or has He in anger withdrawn His compassion? Then I said, 'It is my grief, That the right hand of the Most High has changed.'

"I shall remember the deeds of the Lord; surely I will remember Thy wonders of old. I will meditate on all Thy work, and muse on Thy deeds. <u>Thy way, O God, is holy;</u> (underline mine). What god is great like our God? Thou art the God who workest wonders; Thou has made known Thy strength among the peoples. Thou hast by Thy power redeemed Thy people, The sons of Jacob and Joseph.

"The waters saw Thee O God; The waters saw Thee, they were in anguish; the deeps also trembled. The clouds poured out water; The skies gave forth a sound; Thy arrows flashed here and there. The sound of Thy thunder was in the whirlwind; the lightnings lit up the world; the earth trembled and shook, Thy way was in the sea, and Thy paths in the mighty waters, and Thy footprints may not be known. Thou didst lead Thy people like a flock, by the hand of Moses and Aaron."

Psalm 77

I have written out this psalm in its entirety because it mirrors so well the mind of a very worried mother. The writer's words could be my own.

Notice the change of heart the writer has, as he begins to concentrate more on God and less on himself. He remembers God's faithfulness in other times of his life. He meditates on what God has done and who He is. He compares the recent acts of God and the ancient acts of God and finds them consistent. Then he pulls back even further and observes God as the enormous creator genius to whom all of nature submits. Finally, he zooms back in to God as the good and loving shepherd of the helpless sheep.

There is nothing more comforting, encouraging or hopeful than to meditate on the huge and holy God we have. When Job begins to question God about what He is doing in his life, God reviews His rule over the creation and asks Job if he could do the job.

When I recall who God really is, and of what He is capable, I have confidence in Him. He made our son Ted by His great design, and He knows every atom in his brain and feeling in his heart. My God is in control of the oceans, the sky, the animals and all that He has made by a word from His mouth. My God has not lost control of my situation. I am a small woman in the Midwest with a son she is presenting to God as her scrambled-up puzzle. Is this same God not able to figure it out? He made the puzzle, He knows how it fits together, and He sees its perfect completion. The puzzle has missing pieces that I can't find. God knows where they are.

I am struck that I underestimate this Holy, perfect God of love, knowledge and power.

As I write this, Christmas is weeks away. Yesterday in church, we sang carol after carol about the mystery of an eternal God who entered time as a vulnerable baby and then left it to finish as a resurrected Savior. I realized again how unimportant is my ever-changing perception of God, when compared to the enormity of His reality. When my thoughts are about Him, they push out the panic of my problems. He shrinks my issues to a size I can grasp and strengthens me to drop them at His royal feet.

Thank You, Lord, that You are bigger than anything else and yet You are concerned and involved with the minutia and cares of my life. Thank You that there is nothing and no one more powerful, more holy, kind or loving than You.

62

Lord, I pray that I will consciously dwell on You. Help me notice how You are in everything. Please help me get my mind off myself, for I am tired of my troubles. "Holy, Holy, Holy, there is none beside Thee, perfect in power and love and purity."[15]

Day 27. Compare and Despair

"Every word of God is pure. He is a shield unto them that put their trust in Him."

Proverbs 30:5 KJV

A network of parents is a valuable storehouse of experience and wisdom. Sharing with each other can be great encouragement. But we can also allow comments from other moms to weigh us down and shrivel our confidence. Be careful how much power you attach to what other parents say. Always take that advice to God first, as your filter and interpreter.

I sat at lunch across from a woman I greatly esteem, and listened to the account of her son's benevolent activities and altruistic ambitions. I left with continued high regard for this mom, and happiness for her son's endeavors, but my heart was heavy because my own son was not in a good place. I concluded that I was much less of a mother than her, because one of our sons was going in the opposite direction from hers. I began to beat myself up with the thought that Ted's struggles were due to my parenting. I should have done more of this, less of that. I should have done everything the way she did it, no matter what that was. I compared and lost the competition.

Later, I learned the other woman's son was suffering great difficulty in several areas of his life at the time of that luncheon. This reminded me that no family, child or mom is perfect, regardless of how they sound or look.

While I do not rejoice in the troubles of others, I cannot believe the lie that tells me I am the only one who struggles with a child and, because I do, that I am a bad mother and mine is a bad child. We can't know the full truth about the lives of families we observe. Some parents are candid about the issues they face with kids who have challenging personalities, circumstances or seasons of life. Others exercise their prerogative of privacy. Some parents are prideful and refuse to admit to others (and quite possibly themselves) that they have problems with their children like everyone else does. I have caught myself, on more than one occasion, saying something boastful about my child or bragging – what I called sharing -- about some incredible act of parenting on my part. Shame on me, because I know how very hard it is for me to hear that from another parent when I feel inadequate about raising my own child.

What I am hoping to learn is this: whether the accounts from other parents are complete, altered or fabricated, I should never react by comparing the other child with my own. Do not draw conclusions, good or bad, about your ability as a parent from the "results" in other families. Ultimately, we need to gauge who we are and who our children are through the eyes of God. Our child's creator does not compare him or her with other teens and, thankfully, He does not determine our worth as mothers on a graded curve. Believe only in God for pure truth, and trust only in Him for your confidence.

Other parents can be a tremendous help to me in raising my children, but I need to understand that they are different from me and their children are different from mine. God understands the uniqueness of my son and He determined that I should be his mom. He has promised to be a shield for me when I trust Him. I must hold up my shield when I am tempted to skew the words of others into a threat to what I know to be true, according to God's perspective.

Thank You, Lord, that You are a wonderful counselor and the filter for my thoughts. You believe in my ability to mother this child of mine. You empower me to do and be something significant, in my own way, in the life of this unique individual.

Lord, I pray that I would be more sensitive in my speech and less sensitive in my emotions. Make me an encouragement to others and less introspective. Let me listen with the mind of Christ, without comparison or ego.

Day 28. Owning His Own

"And I will give them a heart to know Me, for I am the Lord and they will be my people, and I will be their God, for they will return to Me with their <u>whole heart</u>." (emphasis added)
Jeremiah 24:7

Although I am sometimes preoccupied with the goal of having my son behave, what I really want is for him to know God, and to love and follow Him. After years of disobedience, our son, Ted moved into a most welcomed season of compliance. Days and weeks passed without incident and we were grateful. But as I read my Bible, I was reminded that I need to be careful not to let behaving be my sole goal for him.

Although Ted was not breaking many rules at the time, he had admitted that he had not reconciled things with God. I continued my urgent daily prayers, because clearly there was a lot of work God and Ted still needed to do. What I want for all of our children is for them to love God with all their heart, mind and soul, and that the world would know that they are His because Christ shows in the way they live their lives.

I was taken in by something while I attended a junior high school leader's retreat that centered on the magnitude of God's love for us. I realized that, in our trouble with Ted, I may have weighed in too heavily on the do's and don'ts of God, the compliance factor, the "you are displeasing to God" tone. Without indulging in guilt or regret, I wish I had centered on God's love for him. It is that love relationship that drives authentic obedience.

Until Ted is personally right with God, my prayers for him should not weaken or wane. Any teenager can comply, but the best for our son – the very best – is for him to entrust himself to His own God and live by His plan. I know that then he will be all that he was intended to be.

Thank You, Lord, that my son's relationship with You is not under my control. Thank you for the knowledge that You want his friendship more than I can know. Thank you that once he reaches for You he will know peace and real fulfillment. In the meantime, I thank you for the blessing of good behavior in any form that protects him.

Lord, I pray that my son would obey You because he loves You. I pray that You would give me what I need to love him the way You do, even in discipline. Let him see Your love in me somehow. Help me to wait for him to have a changed heart that longs to know You.

Day 29. Who Has Your Back?

"My Servant will justify the many, as He will bear their iniquities. Therefore, I will allot Him a portion with the great, and He will divide the booty with the strong; because He poured out Himself to death, and was numbered with the transgressors; yet He Himself bore the sin of many, and interceded for the transgressors."

Isaiah 53:11b-12

I sat one day on our piano bench, listening to the closing prayers of mothers gathered in my living room. Our monthly Moms in Touch group was praying for the teachers, administrators and students in our high school. One mother talked to God about the disturbing language she saw her son use on a school-made videotape. Others joined in with tears to pray for their children who were not making good choices. After we closed our prayer time, Mary Ann was eager to share the above Bible passage that had helped her. "Please let me share this. I have loved this verse. When my son breaks my heart I turn to this and say, 'Lord, do this for my son. Intercede for him.'"

Early in these verses, we see Jesus' death prophesied and God's plan to substitute His perfect Son for our wrongdoing. As my friend Mary Ann pointed out, Jesus intercedes for the ones who disobey. "Do you know that Jesus goes before the Father on behalf of our kids who rebel?" she asked us. To intercede means "to act between parties with a view to reconciling differences."[16] And you thought you were your child's only source of prayer. Jesus is communicating to the Father on your behalf about your child. He was "numbered with the transgressors" when He took on the world's sin by "bearing our iniquities" on the cross. Not only that, He prays for the transgressors – for you, me, and our children. What an incredible truth.

While it is so difficult to watch a child say no to God's way and yes to a different way, it is reassuring to know that Jesus Himself takes on full responsibility to present our child before the Father. Day after day I have said, "Jesus, don't forget." He does not.

68

The picture of Jesus presenting God with the weight of our children on His heart makes me think of the earlier verses in Isaiah 53. "Surely our griefs He Himself bore, and our sorrows he carried." The side reference of the NASB Bible version says, "our pains He carried." I picture Jesus carrying my tub of concerns in His arms and my load of pain on His back as we walk to the Father together. He unpacks them in front of God and makes my case. I trust Him to be thorough.

Thank You, Lord, that You are involved in my prayers. You intercede for my much-loved child. You intercede for me. My concern is so much your concern that You offer to carry it. Thank You for dying for me and living for me.

Lord, I pray that one day my child will realize how much it cost You to take on their personal sin and the sin of the world. I pray he will understand that You did it for the love of him.

Day 30. I AM. You're Not.

"Then Job answered the Lord, and said, 'I know that Thou canst do all things, and that no purpose of Thine can be thwarted. "Who is this that hides counsel without knowledge?" 'Therefore I have declared that which I did not understand, things too wonderful for me, which I did not know.' "Hear now and I will speak; I will ask Thee, and do Thou instruct me."'

Job 42:1-4

My oldest son John left for a Christian conference for college students in Minneapolis. Because I wanted to pray for his time there, I looked up the schedule of events on the internet and found this update on the conference home page:

> As the evening session convened, anticipation was high for what the Lord would do. Bryan Loritts led off with a picture of I AM: God's sovereignty and goodness even in the midst of difficult circumstances. Dynamic worship ended the evening, as students anticipate three more days of seeking the Lord's face.
> I AM: God's sovereignty and goodness even in the midst of difficult circumstances.

I attended the same type of conference 27 years ago. I wish that I could be there now to hear this particular talk. I could learn something in my middle-aged walk with God.

Last night, our son Ted's two-year relationship with his girlfriend ended, and I wondered, "God, is this Your plan for him? Are You sure you're overseeing this? Everyone in our family is sad and I personally am wondering if You're on top of it." And so I had gone off sniffling to grocery shop and begun a mental list of "new things to worry about related to this break-up."

About five aisles through the supermarket, it occurred to me that I could trust God with this situation about which I can do nothing. I could ask His counsel regarding my part. I could entrust to Him the heart of my son and the separate heart of his former girlfriend. I could trust God with the difficult void Ted will experience for awhile. God never takes a well-deserved vacation from being in control. He is always good. In every situation, He is deserves my trust because He is trustworthy. He tells us not to worry and not to be afraid. I force my mind to focus on these truths.

In our day and age without kingdoms or monarchs, what does that churchy word "sovereignty" mean? When I looked it up, I was intrigued by what I found: "1. Supreme excellence or an example of it. 2. a. supreme power especially over a body politic; b. freedom from external control: autonomy; c. controlling influence."[17]

If I believed all of this – God's sovereignty and goodness in the midst of difficult circumstances – I would be free. Before he left for the conference, John shared Proverbs 30:5 with me: "Every word of God is tested; He is a shield to those who take refuge in Him." I imagine God would say, "Take Me at My word and see if it is solid. Go ahead, bring it on. I wish you would." Well, I might just have to do that.

Oh, it would be grand to stow away with John to the conference and hear more about God's sovereignty and goodness in difficult circumstances, but I have all I need to go on here -- 30 years of seeing it and an invitation to believe it. He is the great and the good I AM.

Many times I think I only have two choices: I can worry, or I can worry a lot. There is a third choice: I could not worry. Why would I need to worry when God is all powerful, excellent in character and judgment, who is not controlled by anything or anyone? Can you believe it for yourself in your circumstances and in the circumstances of your son or daughter? We have the choice.

Thank You, Lord, that You are on the throne and I am not. There is nothing over which You do not have power and no situation in which You are helpless. Above all, You are good. Thank You that in difficult circumstances, we can know that You are still good and in complete control.

Lord, I pray that I will remember to believe You. Please help me to exchange my panic and worry for Your promise to guard my heart and mind with peace that is beyond understanding. Be ruler over the life of my son. Work out Your plan in his life.

Day 31. "A" For Effort

"Better is a little of the righteous than the abundance of many wicked. ... The steps of a man are established by the Lord; and He delights in his way. When he falls, he shall not be hurled headlong; because the Lord is the One who holds his hand."

Psalm 37:16 and 23-24

Do you ever rate yourself by comparison to other mothers? Do you listen, as I do, to moms tell about the memory-making traditions and activities they do with their children and feel yourself get smaller as you voluntarily descend down the ladder into the barrel bottom of crummy mummies? We women have this insipid habit of comparing up and comparing down. Sometimes we think "hey, our family is a prototype of everything good in the world compared to that zoo of dysfunction." Then we read perky Christmas letters of joyous perfection and conclude that we were the inspiration for the Simpsons.

I remember being at a conference as a young mom, and hearing a lovely young mother describe their family advent wreath lighting ritual. It was tender. It was moving. I tried it at my house. When I announced my plans to my husband as I removed the wreath and colored candles from the craft store bag, I detected a skeptical look on his face. I found his look irritatingly discouraging. Actually, it was just realistic.

Perhaps the difference was that the mom speaking at the conference had three girls, while I had three boys, or that her children were well-behaved and mine were raised by wolves. In any event, when the craft-making started, the fighting began. The shoved-in candles snapped, the hollering middle child burned his finger on the match and the Styrofoam wreath was manhandled to flaky pieces. I tearfully abandoned the whole thing and left the room. On the way past my husband, I saw a look of melded sympathy and amusement.

I have attempted to do a lot of good things with my children over the years. Some of them have failed, but I have provided the best environment I could with what I had to work with (including my own failings) and the mix of people involved. I know now, although I don't always choose to believe it in my low moments, that what seem like small attempts to do good things, however lamely they end, are valuable to God. He gives me a high five and a slap on the back when I come off the field after a fumble. I believe He's proud of me for my feeble attempt to do my job well.

God knows I will fall. When I do, He holds my hand so that, as the verse says, I "will not be hurled headlong." If a child never tried to walk, he or she would not get anywhere at all. When they step and fall, get up and step and fall again, they eventually progress to the other side of the room. What parent is not delighted at this wobbly and awkward attempt? What parent is not happy to take the child's hand so that he will not fall down the stairs head first?

My husband likes to encourage me, in my neurotic moments of self-loathing, that we have our own personality as a family. We have as many successful traditions as the next family. The next family has as many well-intentioned activities that end in disaster as we do. This is not a competition and there is no standard to which we are held accountable except to do our best with God's help. We're human, we're sinful, we have dislikes and likes and so do our children. We make mistakes. We can have the sense of humor that God has, realize the delight He has in the small things we do to please Him, and give ourselves just a fraction of the grace God gives us for trying.

Thank You, Lord, that You look at our hearts, not our success. What we envision as mothers often just doesn't work. Thank You that what matters to You is our effort. You hold my hand as I awkwardly walk this walk of motherhood. Thank you that the sincerity of my feeble attempts brings You joy.

Lord, I pray that I will not spend time honing in on what I have done wrong or failed to accomplish. I want to remember that my purpose is to draw attention to You and not to myself. Let me be able to say that I tried very hard and leave the results to You.

Day 32. Mind Over Matter

"Finally brethren, whatever is true, whatever is honorable, whatever is right, whatever is pure, whatever is lovely, whatever is of good repute, if there is any excellence and if anything worthy of praise, let your mind dwell on these things. The things you have learned and received and heard and seen in me, practice these things; and the God of peace shall be with you."

Philippians 4:8, 9

I opened Ted's closet last night and on the floor I found a videotape by a comedian of whom I strongly disapprove. I felt sick again. I felt as though he had sunk to a new low, and I went to bed saddened. Because my son still resides in our home under our authority, I left him a note telling him the tape must be removed from our house immediately.

I wondered what I should say to him.

This morning, when I prayed about this videotape and the other media that he ingests, I was tempted to burrow into a hole of self-pity and alarm. I thought of God's Word. I think of how Ted should fill his mind with things good and lovely, of things pure and excellent, things of good reputation and worth praising. Tears came, and my old friend named discouragement came charging at me again.

Then it occurred to me that God's words about our thought lives are not written to my son alone. They are also for me. I am to dwell on good things. I am to think of truth and things which are right. My mind will not find peace by nestling into a burrow of darkness. I don't belong there any more than does my son.

What is true is God. His Word is true. His promises are true. He is all goodness. He is lovely and worth praising. If I keep going, I can see that when my mind is set on God and what He says, light shines between the cracks in the dungeon walls. I can walk up the dingy stairs to a wide open place where the stale air becomes fresh.

God's Word is for me. God is for me. He is for our son. I mentally laid the coarse videotape at His feet this morning and spoke to Him about the talk I must have with Ted. Yes, I dread it, but an anxiety-ridden discussion with my own mother went surprisingly well yesterday. Did God help me in that situation? He did. I consciously decide that He can and will help me again.

But when and how can the end result of these challenges with Ted be good? I want to know that someday there will be a happy ending to the trouble we have now. However, I can only have what I need for this moment. I don't get to see down the banquet table, only at the plate which is in front of me. I take the step to set my mind on what is true, honorable, right, pure, lovely, what is of good repute, excellent and worthy of praise.

Thank You, Lord, for showing me things I need to see. This keeps me in reality which keeps me praying. What Your Word outlines for my son to do and be, I must do and be. Those words were written for me, too, and what I desire to see in my son I must strive for in myself. When I look for things good and lovely, I'll find them.

Lord, I pray for the peace that passes understanding. Whether today is a good or a bad day, Your offer to guard my heart and mind in Christ Jesus is always available. The choice is mine. Let me choose this day to dwell on that which is good, in the world and in my son. Let my thoughts rest there.

Day 33. Fret Not

"Fret not yourself because of evildoers, be not envious toward wrongdoers. For they will wither quickly like the grass, and fade like the green herb. Trust in the Lord, and do good; dwell in the land and cultivate faithfulness."

Psalm 37:1-3

When we had been married only a few months, my husband and I began working with teenagers in our church. We met Rocky Fancher at that church, a charming sixty-something big man with a white crew cut brightened by his deep tan. Retired from a lifetime as an encyclopedia salesman, Rocky and his wife Betty were in their fourth decade investing in the lives of young people. One Sunday night at our youth group meeting, Rocky spoke slowly to the students in his signature deep and gentle voice. "Fret not" was the title of his message that evening, delivered from an overstuffed chair in somebody's living room. Rocky and Betty's oldest adult son had died three months before in a Colorado car accident. With a slight pause to wall up the tears filling his bright blue eyes, he went on reading from his Bible to the students seated on the floor. "Cease from anger, and forsake wrath; fret not yourself, it leads only to evildoing."

My husband and I quote those two words to each other from time to time – fret not. When we say them, we think of Rocky. The words serve as a sweet memory of a man we loved, and as a reminder to imitate the fret-not obedience that Rocky Fancher lived even through his darkest hour. But should we fret when we feel a child is slipping away? Don't we deserve to fret in the serious risk of losing a child to another world? No. Rocky lost a child altogether, which is imagined fear realized. Rocky grieved, but he fretted not.

Oswald Chambers tell us: "Fussing always ends in sin. We imagine that a little anxiety and worry are an indication of how really wise we are; it is much more an indication of how really wicked we are. Fretting springs from a determination to get our own way. Our Lord

76

never worried and He was never anxious, because He was not out to realize His own ideas; He was out to realize God's ideas."[18]

As well as I think I know Ted, my ideas for what is best for his life, what he needs to learn and in what order, are not necessarily in sync with God's. I like to be in control, to a point. When things are out of control, I would rather someone else take charge, as long as that person knows what they're doing. At the final hour, I prefer to throw that responsibility on an all-knowing God and say "far be it for me to interfere." I almost feel God looking at me over His shoulder and saying "okay, then fret not."

Thank You, Lord, for relieving the pressure I feel. I know that You know I sometimes need to grieve, but I never need to fret. I really am thankful that I am not in control if You are. If things do not seem right or fair or even better, that does not mean that You are not orchestrating Your will.

Lord, I pray for my child's pathway to be one that leads him to You. Whatever route he needs to take, let it happen if he ends up surrendering to You. As I get to know You better, please show me more and more about Yourself that compels me to unclench my teeth, open up the tight grip of my hands and fret not.

Day 34. Free Will Versus Freedom

"...but we speak God's wisdom in a mystery, the hidden wisdom, which God predestined before the ages to our glory; the wisdom which none of the rulers of this age has understood; for if they understood it, they would not have crucified the Lord of glory; but just as it is written, *'Things which eye has not seen and ear has not heard, and which have not entered the heart of man, all that God has prepared for those who love Him.'"*

I Corinthians 2:7-9

My journal entry one January day read: "In a way Lord – today anyway – I think it's kind of sad (You already know the word 'mean' is in my head although I know You are not mean) that You made people capable to choose their own way. In doing that, "people" translates to not just a neighbor or an acquaintance but our own son. When Ted does not choose You, I look to You to do something. Make him choose You! You are able, but to be consistent with Your creation of free will in man, will You? Will You show Yourself to him in a special way? Will you surround him with circumstances that pull him toward You? Will you reveal to him his undeniable need for You? Will You make Yourself irresistible to him? Can You in staying with Your own design, do anything to persuade our son to follow You?

"Actually, yes You can. You can because You insist on having freedom to do what You want. You can because it is Your prerogative to be mysteriously consistent and yet simultaneously retain the authority to bring about what You want, how You want. My desired result is Your desired result. We are on the same side. You are fighting for me. My prayers can move You and so moved, You move heaven and earth to accomplish all You want to give Your loved children.

"So yes, You can save my son with a free will. I ask You to do it."

"But as for me, I would seek God. And I would place my cause before God;

Who does great and unsearchable things, wonders (miracles) without number." Job 5:8

Thank You, Lord, that I can't fully understand You. Gerhard Tersteegen said, "a comprehended God is no God at all." Thank You that I can know You. You and I are friends, but we are not equals. I appreciate the fact that You will do what You want and still stay consistent. I know that You want my son to follow You – I do too.
Lord, I pray that You will show Yourself to my son. I pray that he will respond. Take away my fear that this will never happen. Center my mind on all that is good and not the bad that I imagine could happen. Give me extra faith this day to trust You so that I can go forward and be useful to others -- ultimately useful to You.

Day 35. Ice Maker, Ice Melter

"He gives snow like wool;
He scatters the hoarfrost like ashes.
He casts forth His ice as fragments;
Who can stand before His cold?
He sends forth His word and melts them;
He causes His wind to blow and the waters to flow."

Psalm 147:16-18

This morning, I asked God for a prayer to pray for my Ted. I looked to the psalms, where I knew I would find imagery written by David, a man after God's own heart. I wanted to pray back to God, something about Him that is true.

I didn't take the time to understand everything about this passage of Psalm 147 but, on this January day, looking at the snowy sparkle of my back yard, God gave me something to say to Him, which is also about Him.

He makes ice and He melts it. He stirs the invisible to motion. It is His alone to move. Who else can move the wind? Who else can confront a mind to change? "The king's heart is like channels of water in the hand of the Lord; He turns it wherever He wishes." Proverbs 21:1

"Lord," I wrote in my journal, "melt the ice with Your word. Stir up the wind of Yourself, powerful and gentle at the same time, and cause it to blow over Ted, a fresh spring-like wind that moves through his hair and is new on his face. Let him feel you softly but persistently coming at him with no obstacles to block You. Begin a current in the waters of his heart. What has seemed stagnant as a murky pond, move with determination towards a living sea where there is clarity and color and life."

Thank You, Lord, for making my child just as he is. I do not always understand the complexities of his nature, but I know he is Your design, in Your image. Thank You that the very characteristics that seem to derail him can be his greatest strengths.

Lord, I pray that just as You have made my child, You would melt in him what is cold toward You. Shift the wind of Your Spirit to blow on him and open the dam he has made to keep You out.

Day 36. Shields Up

"The Lord is my strength and my shield; my heart trusts in Him, and I am helped; therefore my heart exults, and with my song, I shall thank Him. The Lord is their strength, and He is a saving defense to His anointed."

Psalm 28:7, 8

I have spent more than a few nights sitting in my living room chair, waiting up for our son, Ted, to come home. Tonight is one of those times when I feel afraid. I anticipate that I will not get answers to the questions I need to ask him. What I don't know will scare me as much as what I do know. In many exchanges between our son and me, his words and anger and even the information he shares have felt like arrows aimed point blank at my chest. I have wanted to go back to the days when bedtime included the reading of books, singing and good-night kisses.

When Batman approaches trouble in the Batmobile, he says "shields up" and a bullet-proof, transparent guard plate rises electronically. I would like to put shields up when I know that Ted and I are entering the danger zone of confrontation.

Still, God is my shield. He is the guard that rises up in front of me, protecting my heart and mind when I do what I need to do. I don't like the confrontational part of motherhood, but it comes with the territory and so I walk through the minefield. I don't do it undefended. God protects me. I feel the force of the blast, but I am not destroyed.

Half of my heritage is a gene pool teeming with bad tempers. There have definitely been disagreements when I continued the legacy. The times I choose to allow God in the situation, I have almost felt like an observer, when the Holy Spirit keeps my fuse from being lit, I do not explode. I cannot choose what comes at me, but I can choose my reaction.

God is a shield or a bulwark. The latter is defined as "a wall-like defensive structure; a strong support, or protection."[19] The arrows come at me, but they can be deflected. I can almost see God standing

82

in front of me, intercepting those arrows. I am shaken, but I am not destroyed.

Thank You, Lord, for being my shield. I know that anything which comes my way cannot penetrate the protection I have in You. You guard my spirit, mind and heart and I gladly stand behind the one who gave His life for me.
Lord, I pray for more trust in You. I pray that how I react to the arrows fired at me will demonstrate love from You and confidence in You. Equip me for this battle.

Day 37. Where Aren't You?

"Thou hast enclosed me <u>behind</u> and <u>before</u>, and laid Thy hand <u>upon</u> me."

Psalm 139:5

"If I take the wings of the dawn, if I dwell in the remotest part of the sea, even there Thy hand will <u>lead me</u>, and Thy right hand will <u>lay hold of me</u>."

Psalm 139:9, 10

"Even though I walk through the valley of death *(also translated, "the valley of deep darkness)* I fear no evil; for Thou art <u>with me</u>; Thy rod and Thy staff, they comfort me."

Psalm 23:4

"Thou dost enlarge my steps <u>under me</u>, and my feet have not slipped."

Psalm 18:36

"And hope does not disappoint, because the love of God has been poured out <u>within</u> our hearts through the Holy Spirit who was given to us."

Romans 5:5

Many people are enthralled by David's description in Psalm 139 of how God made him. As I read through this psalm on a certain difficult day, I noticed something else.

I am fascinated by the emphasis on God's encircling presence. God isn't just "there" for me. He is not just a cosmic existence who zooms in and out at my beckoning. God has got me surrounded. He is within me. When I asked Him to come into my life as my Savior and Lord, He entered into the heart of me where He now lives. God is not an aura around us. He is so close, so involved, that His hand leads me and His right hand "will lay hold of me."

When I am facing confrontation or fear, He is in front of me, behind me, above and below me, next to me, inside me and standing with His one hand leading me and the other on my shoulder for reassurance. Is there more for which to ask? Yes, the ability to do something. He is able to work and to act. He changes the course of nature, of history and of individual lives.

"O Lord God of hosts, who is like Thee, O mighty Lord? Thy faithfulness also surrounds Thee." Psalm 89:8

God surrounds us; faithfulness surrounds Him. In His closeness is all security. My oldest son John likes this song lyric, in which the writer says about God in his life, "out of the noise I could hear you breathing.[20]" That's how close He is, a breath, a touch, a thought away.

Thank You, Lord, for being the great "I AM" of the universe and being as near as a heartbeat. Thank You that You are surrounded in faithfulness.

Lord, I pray that, in tense and frightening times, in worry and in pain, I would remember that You have Your hand on my shoulder. You are whispering words of love in my ear and filling me with wisdom and power. When my knees buckle, hold me up and put my feet in a secure place.

Day 38. Not in My Job Description

"The steps of a man are established by the Lord; and He delights in his way. When he falls, he shall not be hurled headlong; because the Lord is the One who holds his hand. I have been young, and now I am old; yet I have not seen the righteous forsaken, or his descendants begging bread. All day long he is gracious and lends and his descendants are a blessing."

Psalm 37:23-26

While in high school, I tried all kinds of things to fill myself up. I lived a double life. I had various interests and accomplishments. I was a cheerleader, editor of the yearbook, on student council and earned all A's my senior year. Teachers liked me and my father thought I was perfect. Still, I felt lost, so I used friends, boys, alcohol and crazy parties in an attempt to fill up the emptiness.

I couldn't wait to go to college to be on my own and pursue my dreams. When I got there, I found it to be all that I had hoped. I loved my classes and the new variety of friends and boys. I loved independence. However, I still found that even the college lifestyle wasn't enough to complete me. Something was missing but I wasn't sure what.

My new roommate, Cindy, quickly became my unlikely friend. I noticed in her, something unusual. I was curious about the way she lived her life, which was so different than mine. She told me that she had a personal relationship with Jesus Christ. I had always loved God, but because efforts like changing churches didn't lead me to a connection with God, I just concluded in high school that I was not the religious type. I didn't know how to know God. I gave up trying.

Cindy and I had many conversations about Christ, who He was and why He came to earth and especially why He died the way He did. I spent several months talking with her and her friends and thinking hard about what they said and showed me about Jesus. One night on my knees in my dorm room I told God, "if You are who You say You are, if You can forgive the things I've thought, said and done, if You can get rid of all this guilt, if You can be trusted with my future and if You can change the things I hate about myself, if knowing and following You secures my place in heaven with You -- because I'm so scared to die -- then I ask You to come in to my life and do it. I believe in You. I want You in my life."

Life was different from that moment on. I have never looked back on the decision to give my life to God. In the decades since I said yes to Christ, never has He let me down. Hard times? Of course. Life doesn't stop happening, but I do life with God, who orchestrated it all the way it was meant to be done under His care and direction.

A few years ago, I sat in church and had this thought, unprompted by anything I can think of that was happening at that moment: "Sarah, God here. You had a spiritual path that led you to Me in your freshman year of college. No one drew that map for you except Me. Between your father's alcoholism and death, your own behavior, your emptiness and all your fears, you were on a collision course with something very bad. I saved you, didn't I? I rescued you, didn't I? I had no help from anyone and no one pushed you into the decision to follow Me.

Now, you have a son who is not interested in Me right now. But he knows how to get to Me when he decides he needs Me. You cannot dictate his spiritual path, just as no one dictated yours. Let Me handle him. You trusted Me with your life 28 years ago. Can you trust me with His?"

God had me there. Good point. We all have our own spiritual paths. No two stories are exactly alike. My son is not me. He was not intended to be an extension of me.

Sometimes I falter in my trust that God will invade our son's life one day. At least I question God about it from time to time. Like water through my fingers, our son's relationship with God is not mine to hold. It never was. I keep asking and trying to let go, and God keeps listening and working His own way. He does not owe me an update or a timeframe. He encourages me through His Word and builds my faith. He keeps all His promises to me. In that, I am filled up.

Thank You, Lord, that my child's relationship with You is not under my control. I know he has the choice to follow You or not follow You.

Still, your will is for everyone to be a disciple of Christ. Thank you for being in charge of my child's path to You.

Lord, I pray again that You draw my son to Yourself in ways only You can. You moved the chess pieces to save me. Help me to show love to my child and those around me. That is my part. I trust You. I believe. Help me in my unbelief.

Day 39. Getting Out of the Woods

"For Thou dost light my lamp; the Lord my God illumines my darkness."

Psalm 18:28

"In Thy light, we see light."

Psalm 36:9b

"But the path of the righteous is like the light of dawn, that shines brighter and brighter until the full day."

Proverbs 4:18

"And this is the message we have heard from Him and announce to you, that God is light, and in Him there is no darkness at all."

1 John 1:5

This February morning, my office window looks out on a gray sky as a backdrop for dull trees hanging onto limp, dead leaves which drip water onto patches of olive-colored muddy ground. Do you sometimes feel like this picture looks? If you had to pick a color to describe your life, would it be gray? Is the forefront dull and murky and does even the foliage drip with discouragement?

Here in Wisconsin, we attribute our dark feelings in February and March to the dismal winters in which we live for almost half the year. It affects us, we say, and how can it not? So it can be with our spirits. When we consistently watch our children wander to places they should not go -- depression, cutting, alcohol and other drugs, frightening friends, eating disorders, rebellion, anger -- we huddle under the clouds right with them day after overcast day. We crave a circumstantial and emotional climate change, a break in the clouds as a few consecutive days of encouragement. We want our children to find a new day, so that we can too.

I sometimes feel that it would be abandoning my child to get out from under his cloud and to absorb my own spiritual light. However, Jesus said, "I am the light of the world." John 8:12. If I depend on my child to change in order for me to find serenity, I am putting my hope in something that guarantees to disappoint. No person, no matter how deeply I may love him or her, has a life purpose to fulfill my needs. God has reserved this for Himself, in order that we may find satisfaction in only Him. Notice that Jesus did not say that He and the Father have light. He said He is light. There is no other source.

I cannot stay under my child's cloud. I am no good to anyone there. I know where I can go. "I will lift up my eyes to the mountains; from whence shall my help come? My help comes from the Lord, Who made heaven and earth." Psalm 121:1, 2.

Thank You, Lord, that You are what I need. Thank You that there are resources and tools available to help me. I am not alone. Other people have been where I am now. I can ask for help and You will be faithful to provide it. Thank You in advance.

Lord, I pray for supernatural deliverance from my sadness. Help me to expect Your help one hour, then one day at a time. If I am looking for my child to get out of the woods before I can be happy, show me how to get out first, right now, and to take the first step toward light. I want to live my life.

Day 40. Joy is Not for Sale

"All my springs of joy are in You."

Psalm 87:7b

While on a walk one day with my headphones on, I listened to a talk by well-known speaker and author Beth Moore. "Don't hand over control of anything in life to anyone but the Holy Spirit," she said. The message to me could not be more direct. Instantly it was apparent to me that I was letting something else have control over my life. I was allowing my sadness over the choices our son was making to manage me. Despair over his actions was overtaking my thoughts, emotions and energy.

I stopped the CD right there. In the difficult talk with God that followed, I told God that I knew I had to face the possibility that our son might never live the life I wanted for him, and that might be his choice. It was, however, not necessary for me to go on lock down in despondency. I had allowed Ted to take the joy from my life. When Ted began to make bad choices, I increasingly let go of the joy in my life.

Internal joy does not mean that I live life on a constant peak of perkiness. Joy is the inner assurance that God is in control of me even when things around me are completely chaotic or tragic. I should never invest my joy in people, things and circumstances. Jesus honestly tells it like it is: "These things I have spoken to you, that in Me you may have peace. In the world you have tribulation, but take courage, I have overcome the world." John 16:33.

Jesus said that we may have peace in Him. In You, God, are my springs of joy, *all* of them. As author Stuart Briscoe explains, happiness comes from happenings. Joy is something different. It is the inner contentment, cemented in an inalterable hope and security that circumstances cannot wear down. I must protect my inner joy and peace.

Thank You, Lord, that I don't have to look for joy any further than my own back yard. It is found all around me in a thousand visuals and gifts and in the stability of You, God, Yourself. Even You were not always happy in Your life here on earth. You cried. You got angry and frustrated. Still, You knew how to get filled up and refreshed. Your joy was in the Father.

Lord, I pray that others would see a deep-seated joy in me. I do not want to give anyone responsibility for my joy except God. Help me choose to live in the understanding that You have overcome tribulation and disappointment. Let ALL my springs of joy be found in You.

Day 41. Panic Attack

"For we are powerless before this great multitude who are coming against us; nor do we know what to do, but our eyes are on Thee."
2 Chronicles 20:12b

I would like to handle crisis the way Jehoshaphat did. Here is what was happening one day in Jehoshapat's life, as recorded in Chapter 20 of 2 Chronicles:

> Now it came about after this that the sons of Moab and the sons of Ammon, together with some of the Meunites, came to make war against Jehoshaphat. Then some came and reported to Jehoshaphat, saying, "A great multitude is coming against you from beyond the sea, out of Aram and behold, they are in Hazazon-tamar (that is Engedi)." And Jehoshaphat was afraid and turned his attention to seek the Lord, and proclaimed a fast throughout all Judah. So Judah gathered together to seek help from the Lord; they even came from all the cities of Judah to seek the Lord. Then Jehoshaphat stood in the assembly of Judah and Jerusalem, in the house of the Lord before the new court, and he said, "O Lord, the God of our fathers, are You not God in the heavens? And are You not ruler over all the kingdoms of the nations? Power and might are in Your hand so that no one can stand against Thee."

In this passage, Jehoshaphat got bad news. The enemy was about to overtake him. His first reaction? Fear. His next move? He turned his attention to the Lord, and had everybody in Judah pray.   Then Jehoshaphat prayed. He reminded himself and his people that God is big. God is able to handle the situation. In fact, God is able to conquer the enemy completely. If you read on in the chapter, you will see Jehoshaphat recall great things God had done in the past.   In his conversation with God, he even threw in a comment about the unfairness of all this: "behold how they are rewarding us". Then Jehoshaphat simply told God that he and his people were powerless against their enemy, that they did not know what to do next, "but our eyes are on Thee."

Have you faced bad news that left you paralyzed with fear? Have you felt as though a great, ugly enemy is marching steadily toward you, and you had absolutely no idea what to do? When faced with trouble, I have paced the floor of my kitchen and said audibly to God, "I don't know what to do! I don't know what to do! Please help me. Please help me. Please help me." I have not always had the presence of mind to review the great things God has done in the past, but I have told him the unfairness of it all. Wouldn't you expect Jehoshaphat to panic? Still, he took his fear to God and allowed the dire situation to be God's problem. Here is what his comrade said to the assembled people after the matter was presented to God:

> Listen, all Judah and the inhabitants of Jerusalem and
> King Jehoshaphat; thus says the Lord to you, "Do not
> fear or be dismayed because of this great multitude,
> for the battle is not yours, but God's."

Whatever attack you are under, it is God's battle. We mothers are at the ready to fight for our children, but in the greater battle for our children's hearts, minds and spiritual well-being, there's a limit to what we can do.

The Israelites were toe-to-toe with the enemy, but they were wise enough to ask God to do for them what they could not do for themselves. Comrade Jahaziel instructed the people in verse 17:

> "You need not fight in this battle; station yourselves,
> stand and see the salvation of the Lord on your
> behalf, O Judah and Jerusalem. Do not fear or be
> dismayed; tomorrow go out to face them, for the
> Lord is with you."

I love how God takes the pressure off of us if we let Him. I love how important it is to God that I not be afraid. I love it that He knows how weak I am, how sick of things I get, how unfair things can be, how enormous is the enemy I face and how easy it is for me to get overwhelmed by the great big thing in front of me. He is my bodyguard, my heart protector.

Thank You, Lord, that I have options when I am afraid. You wait at the ready to step in and fight the battle that I cannot win on my own. Thank you for the words stuck on my refrigerator, "Faith is the refusal to panic."

Lord, I pray that You will make me a person who reacts like Jehoshaphat. If I need to remind myself and others of the victories You have won in the past, bring them to my lips. I will suit up and arm myself, but be my champion. Do what I cannot, and fight for my child and our family.

Day 42. Over-Feeding Worry

"Be anxious for nothing, but in everything by prayer and supplication with thanksgiving let your requests be made known to God. And the peace of God, which surpasses all comprehension, shall guard your hearts and your minds in Christ Jesus."

Philippians 4:6, 7

Worry, the possibilities to do it are endless. Some of us moms indulge daily in a smorgasbord of things over which to agonize. There are just not enough hours in the day to worry about everything we need to worry about.

Have you ever caught yourself circulating an issue around and around in your head only to arrive at the beginning for the zillionth time? This morning, I read through some notes from a seminar at which I had jotted down this simple statistic: "Ninety percent of things we worry about never happen." Winston Churchill said: "When I look back on all these worries, I remember the story of the old man who said on his deathbed that he had had a lot of trouble in his life, most of which never happened."

I don't want the image of a nervous, hand-wringing, brow-furrowed mom to be my legacy. "Don't worry, Mom! I can take care of myself," Ted says. "Oh, really," I think. "You're approaching graduation with a D- in math. You're going out to meet with friends who are in trouble themselves. Your boss called, and it's the third time you've forgotten your schedule. What are the pills I found in your pocket? The last time we went out of town you threw a party. Your eyes don't look normal today."

It's easy to say "don't worry," but we know the temptation is very real. Pushing a looming threat to the back burner of our minds is not easily done. My husband's advice on how to fall asleep quickly is to "think about nothing." It works for him, but I can't imagine for the life of me how it is accomplished. My brain, by nature, abhors a vacuum.

God, in His amazing practicality, knows that for moms, abandoning worry is a colossal challenge. He has a wonderful suggestion for us;

when you empty your mind of worry, fill it with prayer. Prayer accomplishes things. It's something we can *do*. When I choose to pray instead of worry, it keeps me busy. It gives me hope. It takes the pressure off of me and puts it on God. He's the only one who can do anything at that moment anyway, so I'm grateful to dump it in His lap.

There is an old saying: "Worry is like a rocking chair, it gives you something to do, but it doesn't get you anywhere." Prayer, on the other hand, is forward movement. The Bible says it accomplishes things. When I pray, it calms me down. I find myself thanking God for things. I pray for the kids who are with Ted. I pray for his safety and that he will make good decisions. When he is at school, I pray for his teachers and his attitude. I pray for my attitude. Almost always, I pray "and God... don't let go of him." In prayer, there is peace and the sweet promise God gives of protection for my heart and mind. Jesus is the lover of my soul and the lover of my child. Worry be gone. Don't distract me from talking with my God.

Thank You, Lord, for the privilege of bringing all our concerns to You. You invite us to leave them with You and walk with a lighter heart and a clearer mind. Thank You for the option to pray. Thank You that prayer works.
Lord, I pray for wisdom to handle my responsibilities. Give me discernment to know what to do and what not to do. Help me build the legacy of being a praying mom, not a worrying mom.

Day 43. I Believe in You

"Great is my confidence in you, great is my boasting on your behalf; I am filled with comfort. I am overflowing with joy in all our affliction. I rejoice that in everything I have confidence in you."

                                        II Corinthians 7:4 & 16

It was my practice, when Ted was in high school, to periodically email his teachers for a status report. He wasn't communicating with us much, so I contacted teachers directly. A young teacher, Mr. Dapelo, sent me a response once in which he wrote "Ted is a remarkable young man." I stared in stillness at that sentence. I came back to it later in the day, and kept the email in my personal folder. The teacher was right, but I had not acknowledged that Ted was a remarkable young man in a long time. I printed the email and left it on Ted's dresser. How much more must those words have meant to him? When was the last time that I had told him that he was a remarkable young man?

Our sons say that half the punishment for things they do wrong is the sheer length of the lectures my husband gives to them. What my husband is sure to do, however, is to give a significant dose of encouragement to the boys in the beginning and end of his talks to them. He reminds them of their talents. He amplifies the gifts that God has given them and raises them up above all the rest of us in the family. He outlines the potential of such a gift or talent and tells them how he has seen God use this quality for good in their lives. His goal is for them to get a glimpse of what is possible, with all that God has given to them.

What could I do to balance out the negative with my son and show him that I do think he's a remarkable young man? Browsing with a friend at a local boutique, I saw a package of tiny cards entitled "I Believe in You." On each card, that statement on the cover opened up to a short, encouraging quote and, on the back, a place to write a word or two and sign it.

Most often it was after an argument or dealing with some infraction that I decided I too needed to end the issue with my son on a note of encouragement. I started to leave one of those cards for him in various places with a love note on the back. I also used the cards if Ted was disappointed or discouraged or if we both knew he had a challenge ahead. They only appeared now and then so as not to flatter, but to solidify to Ted that I was more than aware there was so much in him that was exceptional. Learning from my husband, I tried to speak affirmations to him and make a deliberate effort to hug or touch him.

"I believe in you" became my theme with Ted. I printed out the words to Steven Curtis Chapman's song "I Believe in You,"[21] written for a graduating child, and pasted them on the back inside cover of the scrapbook which I presented to him at his graduation. When card shopping, I would look for greeting cards that said "I believe in you" to leave for him from time to time. It was a very accurate and appropriate phrase for that difficult decade between us.

In my dog-eared copy of <u>When Mothers Pray</u>,[22] I read about a mom who was in a season of discouragement with her son. She struggled in prayer for him until she decided to hone in on a good quality in him and focus on that. She prayed for God to strengthen that quality in her son, to use it for good in his life and to help her appreciate him more and better.

A young person needs to know that, when the world may have given up on him, his mom, dad, grandma, grandpa, or teacher still believes and always. We know what's inside of them. We have seen it and we believe.

Thank You, Lord, that You believe in each one of us. The potential You have planted in our children never leaves them. Thank You for reminding us to believe in them too.

Lord, I pray that You would use the encouragement I try to give my son and store it in him. Multiply it and make it last in his heart so he knows that, even if he stops believing in himself, he will know that I still do.

Day 44. Buck up

"Have I not commanded thee? Be strong and courageous! Do not tremble or be dismayed, for the Lord your God is with you wherever you go."

Joshua 1:9

"But as for me, the nearness of God is my good... ."

Psalm 73:28

In less than one hour, I have to go to a meeting. The thought of it is making me almost sick with anticipation, and I wish I had never set it up in the first place. I am exploring an employment opportunity. Now I wish I had controlled the impulse that led to the appointment. I am afraid.

In the meantime, I consider the verse above. Go out with strength and courage. No need to be shaky because God is going along with you. Could that also be for me this moment? I've tried to absorb the same truth before meetings much more difficult than a job interview. Many of those times involved our son Ted.

I always felt anxious before Ted's school conferences. I never knew exactly where he stood with any teacher. He might receive an A or an F. Teachers adored him or they were perturbed by him. He amused or exasperated them. You just never knew what you would get.

God, in His kindness, usually arranged at least one class in which the teacher really enjoyed Ted and could tell me a positive thing around which I greedily clenched my hands. Reports on the opposite end of the spectrum would cause me to walk out to my car at the end of the evening searching my parenting bag of tricks for a motivational tool that we hadn't used yet. On the way home, I would debate about whether or not to inform my husband about the most recent academic wild card our son had played. Sometimes I would just use that time in the car to flush out the tears.

Maybe you must go to a court date with your child. Maybe you have to visit him in jail. Maybe you're just anticipating a silent car ride full of tension after you pick him up from somewhere. Should you risk annoying your child by chattering on? If you say anything, no matter how innocent, will that spiral into an argument that races back to sad silence? Just as the anticipation of an exciting birthday party can be half the fun, so the anticipation of something heart-wrenching can be half of the agony. This is when God steps in and says, be strong and courageous. We're doing this together.

"So what if God goes with me?" you might ask. "I could as easily have an inanimate object in the back seat. That does me no good." Ah, but you forget His power. You forget who God is. He is an active God, a working God, a giving God, a powerful God. "God is able to make all grace abound to you, so that in all things at all times, having all that you need, you will abound in every good work." II Corinthians 9:8 NIV.

The nearness of God is your good. The power of God is your confidence. The love of God is your message. His love for both you and your child is off the charts.

Remember those "can you find it" picture puzzles in *Highlights* magazine? Within a complex illustration of a scene filled with clutter, there were objects drawn in the detail of the image. They were not behind anything or hidden. You just needed to look carefully. In the same way, God is not hiding. Maybe you need to look for Him but He is not elusive. He is right there with you. His power comes with Him.

Thank You, Lord, that where I go, You go also. Thank You that, when I get there, You are able and willing to enable me to face whatever will happen. It is absolutely possible, with this knowledge, for me to be strong and courageous.

Lord, I pray to relax in the confidence that I am not alone. I want to talk to You, call on You and rely on You when I don't know what to do or say or when I am so unhinged that I want to run away. Let me anticipate victory and not disaster, knowing that whatever happens, You are over the outcome.

Day 45. Something from Nothing

"...even God, who gives life to the dead and calls into being that which does not exist."

Romans 4:17

As we walked down the corridor of the mall, I put my hand on my son's shoulder and said with conviction and an element of resignation, "Honey, when you stay at home over a Saturday night, you don't have to go to church on Sunday. Now that you're in college, you can decide. I want you to love God, not love church."

Months earlier, when he was a college freshman and home on weekends to see his girlfriend, I had woken him up for church and explained that it just wasn't in me to leave a sleeping child at home on Sunday morning. He understood, got up, and slept in the pew instead.

On this particular day in the mall, I wondered "Is this expectation accomplishing what I wish it would?"

Our family rule was that everyone goes to church as long as they are living at home. Our son was living at home on weekends, but recently had begun driving the hour back to his dorm every Saturday night in order to, I assumed, skip church. At the mall, he protested to me that it was not to avoid church that he returned to school on Saturday night. Whatever the reason, I felt the need to release him from the regulation and focus on the relationship instead.

A year earlier, I disapproved when some friends let their high school son who was not the least bit interested in church spend Sunday mornings sleeping in. Although I would still maintain that our high school children need to adhere to the house rules, I better understand our friends' standpoint now. Is it possible that certain forced behavior does more damage than freedom of choice? I wish I knew the answer to that question. I became willing to at least address it and edit the rule book.

My pure motivation to make him go was that he might hear something in church that would move him toward the Lord. How would he get any spiritual input if he did not hear Christian teaching at least one hour a week? It scared me to think that his disconnect from hearing the Bible would leave him void of Godly influence in any form.

My impure motivation was rooted in pride. We are a church-going family, involved and visible to others, and I wasn't willing to attend minus a child. "It must be hard to be in a church community and have a child who isn't walking with God," our new youth pastor said empathetically to me when I described our situation. I was surprised how quickly tears came before I acknowledged that it was. Evidently he's heard of the judgment we pronounce on each other.

My pride has been deflated to almost nil at times, and that's not necessarily a bad thing. Mostly, I'm sad that our son, Ted, has voluntarily missed so many fun opportunities our other sons have had. He forfeits so much God offers him by not letting God love him and lead the way.

I heard an Atlanta pastor speak about intimacy with God. A loving relationship with God, he explained, is not defined by church-going. It's not about the practice of religion. It's about a friendship, a love, with Jesus Christ. This is what I want for my son, not an obligated ritual of attendance or a guilt-driven practice of should-do's. Attending church is the result of loving God, not the meaning of it.

In his life-applicable book, Mere Christianity, C. S. Lewis says,

> He (God) works on us in all sorts of ways; not only through what we think our "religious life." He works through Nature, through our own bodies, through books, sometimes through experiences which seem (at the time) *anti*-Christian. When a young man who has been going to church in a routine way honestly realizes that he does not believe in Christianity and stops going – provided he does it for honesty's sake and not just to annoy his parents – the spirit of Christ is probably nearer to him then than it ever was before. But above all, He works on us through each other.
>
> Men are mirrors, or 'carriers' of Christ to other men. Sometimes unconscious carriers. This 'good infection' can be carried by those who have not got it themselves. People who were not Christians

themselves helped me to Christianity. But usually it
is those who know Him that bring Him to others. [23]

This has been true in my own life. Besides the supernatural love of my roommate freshman year in college, I found myself believing Christianity more and more as I debated it with an adamantly agnostic professor. Why, I wondered, was I now defending that which I had abandoned in high school as irrelevant?

God is able to breathe life into something which, moments before, did not exist. It takes faith to believe that. In my overestimation of how I can help God, assuming He wanted my assistance, I'd like to create the environment in which He will work in Ted's life. I want to position things just right in order to make it possible for God to do His miracles. I want to assist Him. I want to control Him. But if I could do that He would cease to be God.

In an article I read on an airplane, a young, astute mother wrote, "I realized that the only thing I could control in my children's lives was the way their parents behaved." If that's true, I don't want to be a stage mother for God. Find me in His audience.

Thank You, Lord, that You can do anything and You can do it all by Yourself. Thank You that You don't require a set-up of manufactured circumstances, elements or atmosphere in order to bring about life from death and something from nothing.
Lord, I pray that You would increase my faith to believe that You are able, without my help, to do what You say You can do. Give life to my child and bring about fullness from emptiness. I acknowledge Your power to do anything, in any way, in any place, at any time, using anyone, everyone or no one in my child's life. You are able.

Day 46. The Tree, the Fortress and the Ship

"Blessed is the man who trusts in the Lord and whose trust is the Lord. For he will be like a tree planted by the water, that extends its roots by a stream and will not fear when the heat comes; but its leaves will be green, and it will not be anxious in a year of drought nor cease to yield fruit."

Jeremiah 17:7, 8

I sometimes associate our children with other images when I pray for them. A tree came to mind as I prayed for Ted one day. I prayed the image of a strong, majestic, solid, soaring tree. The above verse was appropriate as my prayer.

The year came when Ted no longer wanted to go on the youth group winter retreat with his church friends. He had formerly loved his time at a rustic Christian camp named Fort Wilderness, but this year he protested. He said he wanted to spend his vacation relaxing with his friends at home. My husband was skeptical about our insistence that he go to camp, but I insisted. Ted acquiesced: "Okay Mom. But I'm not going next year." We were taking one day at a time in dealing with him anyway, so I could live with that.

He left for the retreat and I begged God to work. "I'm so on the line here Lord," I told God. "Please be big in his life this week. I need You to make this good in whatever way You define good because, if it's not, I'm in trouble." Every day I prayed with the image of the tree in mind. "Grow him just one inch today. If he doesn't grow up, grow the roots down. Strengthen them and plunge them deep. Let those roots hold fast to what he is hearing."

I prayed for the speakers, the singing, the food, his cabin mates, his leaders, the broom ball tournaments, the pranks and hang-out time. I asked God to grow even a millimeter concentric ring in that tree trunk, well aware that trees like this grow slowly.

Every day on my walk during the time when Ted was at camp, I would pray the tree. "I pray that one day he will give his life over to you, body and soul. Make roots to support what is above the surface so when the winds of testing and trouble comes, it, he, will withstand the force." Another day I might pray that the leaders, speakers and friends at the retreat would water the tree. "Let them saturate him with love and kindness and influence for good, Lord. Pour it out, rain it down, and irrigate his soul with Your Word and Yourself so he can soak in something of You."

I prayed with the future in mind, "Father, I want my son to yield fruit one day that changes the world. I want his leaves to be green and lush so that people will be drawn to You because of his life. As I prayed for the recreational activities, I would ask, "Let the sun shine down bright on the tree and nourish it with laughter and fun. Grow my son in this same image You have put in Your word."

Ted's feedback from the retreat was everything for which I had hoped. There were peer conversations late into the night about spiritual things and meaningful discussions with his small group leader. He told us funny stories about the broom ball competition and pranks on girls. At times, he caught himself enjoying it too much in front of me. "I'm still not going next year," he said. Still, during those four days, I thought to myself, God had given me what I had asked of Him.

I still pray the tree image. I believe God for the life of a man described in Psalm 1: "...and he will be like a tree firmly planted by streams of water, which yields its fruit in its season, and its leaf does not wither; and in whatever he does, he prospers."

As I pray for our older son John, I think of a great structure, a fortress, a castle where the foundation is carefully built with rock. I ask God, as the builder, to make it reliable and unshakable. As the walls of his years go up, I ask Him to construct them with skill and care, brick by brick, cemented with the mortar of His Spirit as a seal.

I pray that my youngest son Peter will be like a grand ship, handsome and stately with quiet leadership, resolute to plunge forward through the dangerous waters of life. I pray he will glide steady and unsinkable with God at the helm as captain.

We mothers dream dreams for our children and wonder, "what if he were president? What if she discovered the cure for cancer?" As I pray that God would exaggerate Himself in my sons, I ask that whatever they become, they would be a meaningful component in God's kingdom; a tree, a fortress, a ship.

Thank You, Lord, that You spoke in metaphors, similes and parables. You used what we know of the world to relate to us. I'm doing the same, God, because I want to dream big dreams for my children and believe that You have a great role for them in Your plan.

Lord, I pray that, as You are glorified by what we see in this world, You would be glorified by the lives of my sons. Make them into men who point people to You.

Day 47. Freshen Up

"So faith comes by hearing, and hearing by the word of Christ."

Romans 10:17

"Do you not know? Have you not heard? The Everlasting God, the Lord, the creator of the ends of the earth does not become weary or tired.

His understanding is inscrutable.

He gives strength to the weary, and to him who lacks might He increases power.

Though youths grow weary and tired, and vigorous young men stumble badly,

Yet those who wait for the Lord will gain new strength;

They will mount up with wings like eagles,

They will run and not get tired,

They will walk and not become weary."

Isaiah 40:28-31

One morning, I sent an email to Courtney, a high school junior whom I befriended on a spring break vacation. She had called me with a question about something she read in her Bible. After our talk, I encouraged her to keep reading, because this is how she grows in her faith. I love it when she picks up the phone to tell me she is excited, confused, exasperated, or discouraged in her walk with God, because it is in those times that she discovers something new about Him.

In my time alone with God this morning, my Bible study referred me to the above passage in Isaiah. These verses are quoted frequently because of their beauty and inspiration. I have heard them many times. It would be easy this morning to fly over them with a "yeah, yeah, yeah," but I stopped to drink them in because today I needed the encouragement. Lingering over the words, I looked for something that was solid and true to stabilize my wobbly life of unwelcome surprises.

I feel the same way about Ted right now as I do about the long winter. On this Wisconsin day in late March, I am waiting for some sign of spring but I don't see it. No sun is visible, not one blade of green grass. The snow is gone and the temperature is crawling up slowly, but that is not enough to pull me out of the bland tedium of this place. I am tempted to believe that this dormancy will never end, and I long for some sign of hope that one day this season will pass.

As I email Courtney, I refer her to Romans 10:17. Her faith will increase as she reads and hears God's Word. I push myself back to Isaiah because it is evident I need some faith of my own.

I read the passion of the writer's voice in Isaiah and he seems to ask me,

> Sarah, do you realize what I am about to tell you?
> Have you ever heard how amazing God is? Read this and be reminded:
> The one and only true God is alive and working. He always was and always will be.
> He is consistent.
> God made the Earth. He is powerful. He is creative. Everything you see around you is because of Him.
> He's not sick of your situation and He's not out of ideas.
> It is nearly impossible to grasp how much He understands how you feel.
> He is able to give you strength to go on when you are exhausted.
> When you feel like a deflated balloon, He fills you with supernatural power.
> Even the strongest young moms wear out and give up,
> But however weak, discouraged or old you are, He will show you something new and original. He will give you brand new energy to wait for Him while He plans to do more than you can ask or think.
> You are more than capable to sprint across the finish line and walk confidently to the judge's booth to receive your ribbon for completing the race.

I am thrilled when Courtney calls me with her questions and thoughts about God. How much more does God love it when we call Him with ours? When I look to see the freshness He is offering me in my wintry place, I have an inkling of how much He cares and what He can do.

Thank You, Lord, that You do not want me to hibernate in a warm, dark hole during challenging times. On days when I want to escape life with a long nap, You promise to renew me. Thank You that there isn't anything I need that You are not willing and able to give me and do in me.

Lord, I pray for You to increase my faith. Lead me straight to Your Word because I know that is where I will find a larger, panoramic view of life. Help me look for it as You lift me up and propel me forward.

Day 48. Faith Over Fixing

"And He said to them, '... for truly I say to you, if you have faith as a mustard seed, you shall say to this mountain, "Move from here to there, and it shall move; and nothing shall be impossible to you."'"
Matthew 17:20

Why couldn't the disciples help a seizure-stricken boy who was brought to them by his father? The Bible does not tell us if they tried plan A, B and C, but something was lacking. Jesus told them it was faith. You don't need much, he said, but you need some. Look for God to do the task, not to yourselves.

We were never intended to be the general contractor of our own problems or the problems of our children. "What am *I* going to do about this?" is not a relevant question. We can't change any person's heart, including our own. Trust me, I have tried. I thought that the right retreats, sermons, youth workers and parental lectures could change Ted's heart. I lined them up and said go, but things seldom worked out as I had envisioned.

When I acknowledge God and say "after You," I exhibit faith. I think the mustard seed of faith that Jesus talked about is not the grandiose statement "I know this will all work out perfectly." Instead I think it is the release of my grip. When you pass the ball to God, anything can happen. He might hold it for a while. He might involve you in the play. He might sideline you. He might use a whole other string of players. He might call a very long time-out. He will, however, never forfeit the game.

The vulnerable words of the simple song below have expressed for me the indescribable feeling of blah-ness that sometimes nibbles away at my hope. It's the "I'm at an impasse" place where apathy and discouragement pitch a tent over me and start setting up camp.

> I can't find the words to pray, I'm a little down today
> Can You help me, can You hold me?
> I feel a million miles away, and I don't know what to
> say

Can you hear me anyway?
What I need is for You to reach out Your hand
You have taught me no matter what, You'd understand.
Lord move in a way that I've never seen before
'Cause there's a mountain in the way and a lock on the door.
I'm drifting away, waves are crashing on the shore
So Lord move, or move me.
I've looked everywhere to find a simple peace of mind
But I can't find nothin' on my own.
So I gotta leave myself behind, take up this cross of mine
Give away everything I hold on to
Lord, I know the only way is through this
But Lord, I know I need You to help me do this.[24]

There is nothing wrong with asking God to move. Once you admit that you are stuck in your faith, or lack of it, shoes glued to the floor, the place to start is with honesty. "I could use even a shred of encouragement today God." Look for Him to speak it to you in your Bible or some other creative way. Many days I see something in my Bible that I have not noticed before. Today, this statement by Jesus in Matthew 7:9-11 struck me:

> ...what man is there among you, when his son shall
> ask him for a loaf, will give him a stone? Or if he
> shall ask for a fish, he will not give him a snake, will
> he? If you then, being evil, know how to give good
> gifts to your children, how much more shall your
> Father who is in heaven give what is good to those
> who ask Him!

My mother loved it when my youngest son would ask her, upon her arrival at our house, "Granny, what do you have for me?" She encouraged him to ask this because she enjoyed delighting him with the treat or small gift she had put in her pocket before she left home. Most times, it was only a simple trinket or candy, but it thrilled him. She had something ready before he even asked.

112

Look for God to encourage you in a way you did not expect. It may have nothing to do with your son or daughter but it's a reminder from Him, "I'm thinking about you." I have seen God smooth something out for me as a parent would do for a disappointed child: free up some time on a jam-packed day or have someone make me laugh hard and deep. Sometimes the encouragement comes as God arranges something to go especially right. I want to nod at Him and say, "I got it." He wants us to know He loves us, and He's there to show us how much.

Thank You, Lord, that You are happy to jar me out of a place of unbelief. Thank You for understanding that I need encouragement to keep going. Thank You for making all I need available at my fingertips in Your Word, where You remind me that You have my back.

Lord, I pray that You will give me wings or wheels to be transported to higher ground. Elevate my spirit and my faith. Be the life preserver I clutch to buoy me up when I'm sinking. Pull me back up on to the boat so we can keep sailing together toward a better place.

Day 49. Sky Writer

"But if the Spirit of Him who raised Jesus from the dead dwells in you, He who raised Christ Jesus from the dead will also give life to your mortal bodies through His Spirit who indwells you."

Romans 8:11

In the middle of a four-hour drive home after visiting our older son in college, I called Ted at home to check in with him. He told me he planned to hang out that night with certain friends. Even though this was his regular group, I knew they were not good for him. My stomach felt sick and my heart backed up in my chest. I don't know what else I expected, but the names he listed always bothered me. I quickly finished our chat to get off the phone and sink into tearful sadness and fear.

Ahead through the windshield, I saw the vivid blue sky in front of me with sparingly few clouds strolling across the wide expanse. In the center of this vastness was a vertical column of cloud, intersected across the upper third by a horizontal spindle of cottony white. The cloud-cross lingered as the following song began on the music to which I was listening at that moment:

> What can take a dying man and raise him up to life again?
> What can heal a wounded soul?
> What can make us white as snow?
> What can fill the emptiness?
> What can mend our brokenness? Brokenness.
> Mighty, awesome, wonderful
> Is the holy cross.
> Where the Lamb laid down His life
> To lift us from the fall
> Mighty is the power of the cross.
> What restores our faith in God?
> What reveals the Father's love?
> What can lead the wayward home?

114

What can melt a heart of stone?
What can free the guilty ones?
What can save and overcome? Overcome.
It's a miracle to me
It's still a mystery
It's a miracle to me
The power of God
For those who believe.[25]

At times, I wonder, "God, can you do this? Am I deluding myself, practicing some kind of wishful thinking that is only a mind game I use to cope?" Then I think of the cross and the power that raised Him up. I think of Him carrying the bulky raw wood on His bloodied back, being motivated through the pain toward His death with these words in His head: "for Sarah," and, "for Ted."

Thank You, Lord, for the cross. It is the difference between a philosophy of life and life-changing power.
Lord, I pray that I will look to the cross when I need a reminder of Your tremendous love for my child and me. After I ponder the cross, walk with me over to the empty tomb. Your Son is not there. He is alive. He walked out for me.

Day 50. A Sprout

"I planted, Apollos watered, but God was causing the growth. So then neither the one who plants nor the one who waters is anything, but God who causes the growth."

I Corinthians 3:6-7

A week ago Thursday, I checked email before bed. Only rarely does Ted write from his college an hour away, but six minutes earlier he had. The subject line read Hey. He said *"Mom, I want to get more involved with God..."*

Ted has taken stock of his life and regrouped off and on over the last six years. It is as though he has opened the door of his life to acknowledge that Jesus is knocking but hasn't really wanted to be in the room with Him alone, and so he let it drift shut again. For whatever reason, the resolution he made, in his own words, didn't take. Wanting God, even becoming, "more involved" with God, is not a sticky note to be slapped on a life and pulled away. It is like a screw in a board, weak and wobbly at first but the more it is twisted in, the stronger it becomes. Someday, it is in deep enough to hold things together.

With escalating boldness these last five years, my faith has pushed me to ask God for something big. I have asked that when my son turns his life over to Him, it would be a commitment like a steel screw in solid wood growing ever deeper, stronger inseparable. I am asking God for the world and not just a small country. The means, the speed and the timing of my son's spiritual transformation is not mine to control. It is mine about which to pray.

I want our son to know Christ, but not so that he'll be a nice person or a moral citizen. Rather, I want him to understand the goodness of God and have an idea of His love. Psalm 38 says "Taste and see that the Lord is good." Psalm 34:8 says "How blessed is the man who takes refuge in Him." When Ted sticks his toe in the water and becomes more involved with God, I hope he decides to dive in. He might, however, walk around the pool a few more times to get up the courage.

116

When I was 19, no one was monitoring my spiritual life. I found out later that two friends were praying for me, but there was no one hovering above me or skulking around, evaluating my every spiritual comment or criticism. Still, God was at work, dictating circumstances, putting people in my path and surrounding me with so many loving Christians that I couldn't help but wonder about this Jesus they knew. When I found out about the relationship with Him that was waiting for me, I thought about it for three months and decided to ask Him into my life to forgive my sins and remake me into what He wanted me to be.

The Christian life is a marathon, not a sprint, author Eugene Peterson reminds us. We want people to make a quick turn-around and then hurry and grow up. People choose to plant poplar trees because of their silver-leafed beauty and fast growth; however, most horticulturists warn that poplars' soft wood and vulnerability to disease makes them less stable and strong than a slower-growing tree.

We cannot pull a plant up through the dirt, and we cannot pull someone through their relationship with God. He had a plan for me, He has one for you and He has one for our children. We can pray for fertile soil with roots that are strong, even if they exist below the surface and we can't see them, or appear to us as dormant for a season. In truth, God is alive in the dormancy.

Thank You, Lord, for using me but not needing me. I like not being in charge sometimes. It's exhausting and much too much responsibility. We do what we can to plant and water but thank You that growth is Your job.

Lord, I pray that I will get out of Your way and not hover over new growth, blocking the sun. Show me how to water encouragement as needed and then recognize that You cause the growth in Your time.

Day 51. Be Astonished

"The oracle which Habakkuk the prophet saw. How long, O Lord, will I call for help, and Thou wilt not hear? I cry out to Thee, 'Violence!' Yet Thou dost not save. Why dost Thou make me see iniquity, and cause *me* to look on wickedness? Yes, destruction and violence are before me; strife exists and contention arises. Therefore, the law is ignored and justice is never upheld. For the wicked surround the righteous; therefore, justice comes out perverted.
'Look among the nations! Observe! Be astonished! Wonder! Because *I* am doing something in your days – You would not believe if you were told.'"

Habakkuk 1:1 – 5

My journal writing says:

> Father, I am fearful that I do not have the storehouse of wisdom for this task. I am ill-equipped to find where the cancer of rebellion is in Ted's heart and I have no idea at all how to treat it.
>
> Words of wisdom are hard to deliver when the hearer is trying his best to stop them with a shield of intentional deafness. He thinks he knows and I don't. Because he doesn't see the consequences, he doesn't think there are any. Lord, even this hour I have no idea what to do. Take my tears and replace them with ideas.
>
> Thank you that Your promises are true. You don't lie to me. You can't lie to me."

I know that God always tells the truth. My friend often quotes what Jesus told His disciples in John chapter 14, "In My Father's house are many dwelling places; if it were not so, I would have told you; for I go to prepare a place for you." Following that verse I have written in my Bible, "Has God ever lied to me?"

If something is not true, Jesus says, I will tell you it's not true. Notice how often Jesus said "I tell you the truth" before He made a statement. Apparently, Jesus was well aware that people would find some things He said difficult to believe. Perhaps He should not have had to emphasize the fact that He told the truth, but he understood our human skepticism. I have frequently convinced myself that the bad things around me are insurmountable and unending. Too often, I become so afraid that I doubt God's promises or power.

God responds by saying that we had better pay attention to Him. He is doing all kinds of incredible things, even as we cower in our fears. When I am afraid, I must consciously stop and look around at what He is doing, so that I can wonder and be astonished. Then I can go back to trusting Him in my circumstances, reminded that He can be depended on to do what He has promised.

Thank You, Lord, that You think it is important that I know that You speak the truth to me. Thank You also that I need only look around me to see astonishing things You are doing.

Lord, I pray that You will not allow me to lose my sense of wonder. Help me to be more observant of You as I go about my day. Remind me to praise You.

Day 52. Applaud Him

"Clap your hands, all you peoples; shout to God with the voice of joy. For the Lord Most High is to be feared, a great King over all the earth."

Psalm 47:1-2

My older son's girlfriend has this delightful practice when she's excited. She claps her dainty little palms in front of her face. We love it so much I have adopted it myself. It's funny that her boyfriend, our son John, often does his own masculine version of the same thing. As he runs up the stairs or walks through the kitchen, we never know when he'll startle us with a series of loud sudden claps and a "whoop! whoop!"

For a number of years, we have spent Spring break in Orange Beach, Alabama. We love the church we attend there. Last Easter, you could not have jammed one more ounce of joy into that place. There was clapping – about 45 minutes of it. We clapped through the songs, the instrumentals, the solos, the baptisms, the Easter declarations and the readings of Scripture. There was no stopping us. He is raised and we must make noise.

John's girlfriend's childlike expression of joy and my son's random enthusiasm teach me that, if you're happy and you know it, clap your hands. Choose to have some joy and to show joy. God must love our clapping, or we wouldn't be encouraged in His Word to do it.

Psalm 98:8 says, "Let the rivers clap their hands; Let the mountains sing together for joy before the Lord; for He is coming to judge the earth; He will judge the world with righteousness, and the peoples with equity." I doubt that the rivers and the mountains were motivated to clap because they were having an exceptionally great day. It was because of who God is.

When she is amazed by God, sometimes Bible teacher Beth Moore tells her daughters, "Let's give God a round of applause," and they do.

In her words, "The more you clap for God, the more He'll show up for an encore."

You may not have had one of those hand-clapping moments for a long time. No matter your heartache, there *is* joy to be found. There is an empty grave, a risen Savior, a loving Father, a hearing and working God and the dawn of each new day, fresh with possibilities and the assurance of hope. Can we at the very least clap because we are deeply loved by God?

My friend Susie has terrible migraines at least a week out of every month. On days when she does not have a headache, she sends me long chatty emails. I rejoice in the emails and her headache-free days. She gave me a plaque for my kitchen when we bought this house. It quotes Emerson: "scatter joy." That is exactly what my friend Susie does.

I rejoice in the cake that comes out clean from the bundt pan, being the first appliance service call of the day, the great shirt I found on sale in my size, the haircut that turns out better than I pictured, the meeting that went right for my husband, the big laugh from a stranger's delightful wit. These are the types of things that, even when I am in a sad day, cause me to say to God, "Thank You giving me that Lord. I got Your love note."

Through the years my husband has quoted Peter Pan and advised one of our sons who is feeling crabby or sad to "find your happy thought." It's that one thing that lifts you up and sets you in flight. Look for that thought and, when you find it, hold onto it.

In our former house, I had a poster on our back door that reminded our family as we left the house to "Choose Joy." As humans, we tend to set up camp on the hard things in life and get comfortable there. The sadness about our son or daughter who struggles tempts us to huddle inside that tent of despondency. Many times, I have closed the tent flap to the sun when I knew I had the opportunity to get out and trust God with what lay ahead. Choose joy, scatter it and clap your hands. If you can't find your happy thought, use this one: God is God; He is alive and at work.

Thank You, Lord, that there is always a reason to be joyful. I know that above the clouds is a sky full of sun. I want to rise up and get

122

some of it. Thank You for the love notes and happy thoughts You send to me each day. I'm looking for them.

Lord, I pray that You will fill me up with enough joy to show to others. Let me be someone who brings a smile. For all the things You do to show love to me, I praise and applaud You.

Day 53. That's What You Are, But What Am I?

"For You formed my inward parts; You wove me in my mother's womb. I will give thanks to You, for I am fearfully and wonderfully made; wonderful are Your works and my soul knows it very well. My frame was not hidden from You, when I was made in secret, and skillfully wrought in the depths of the earth; Your eyes have seen my unformed substance; and in Your book were all written the days that were ordained for me, when as yet there was not one of them."

Psalm 139:13-16

One day, I wrote in my journal, "Just when I seemed to have found my sea legs, I am unsteady again."

A sweet young mom friend had just visited me. She home schools all her kids, and has developed many necessary house rules that she and her husband uphold to protect them and maintain their innocence. I commend her for that. I have already lost many of those battles with my son, and only the courage God gives me keeps me from surrendering the fort.

I continue in my journal entry, "She is so thrilled with how she is raising her kids and all her plans for the future. Maybe we should have home schooled our boys. But that is not our family culture. I don't think it ever occurred to me."

When I opened the door to comparison, I allowed self-doubt and false guilt to rock my confidence. I turned this dear young mom's enthusiasm into a message to myself that I was a bad mom.

Have you looked back to second guess yourself? Maybe you scan your decisions and conjure up regrets, as you compare the way you have mothered your children with someone else who seems superhuman. I sometimes do. "I shouldn't have cared so much about this. I should have insisted on that. I never should have allowed that. I was too slack on this and too strict on that." The list could go on forever. At some point, I have to abandon the guilt ship and swim toward reality.

I love the new thought God planted in my head a long time ago, when I was entertaining regrets like they were old friends coming for dinner. God knew our family before our children were born. God knew that I would love field trips, but not playing on the floor. He knew that my husband would not care much about athletics, but would enjoy reading to the kids and building with Legos. He knew that my mother would give the boys pretend guns, and their other grandmother would give them educational toys.

Our financial status, personality types, tastes and family baggage were all well known to God before we were born. He placed these children in this family by His design. God works wonders with what He has.

I remember sitting in a conference as a young mother in which a speaker told us, "You are the perfect mother for your children." Even as I waited for her to name me as the exception, I began to realize the freedom in that statement. With all my faults, God chose me to be the mother of these three boys, and them to be my children. It's not a perfect match, because I'm not perfect nor are they, but it is exactly the way it's supposed to be.

My husband and I have noted that the people we envisioned marrying were nothing like either of us. He dated tall women with long legs and dark hair. I am the opposite. I liked party boys with a crazy sense of humor. He is a stay-at-home, intellectual Dane who lets me be the funny one. Yet, we marvel at how God brought us together, and it works, as much as it can with imperfect people.

Have you thought that you're a brown sock and your son or daughter is a blue one? Realize that what your child needs is not someone like him or her, but someone who is exactly who you are. You were chosen for your position.

Thank You, Lord, that You design families and that no two are alike. Sometimes I feel sorry that my children got me, but the truth is that I'm supposed to be their mom. Thank You that You have always known the weaknesses in our family, and You are capable to work your own design.

Lord, I pray that every day You will fashion me into a better mother. I don't want to question Your wisdom in assigning me this role, but I do want to tap into Your wisdom to do it well.

Day 54. God's Speed

"I will stand on my guard post and station myself on the rampart; and I will keep watch to see what He will speak to me, and how I may reply when I am reproved...For the vision is yet for the appointed time; it hastens toward the goal, and it will not fail. Though it tarries, wait for it; for it will certainly come, it will not delay."

Habakkuk 2:1, 3

I often think of what poet Theodore Roethke wrote: "Deep in their roots, all flowers keep the light." When it is time, the light that has photosynthesized feeds growth. I hope that what Ted learned about God when he was little will be useful to him in finding his way back to God. I hope that, deep in his roots, he has kept the light.

Certainly, a farmer has known the hardship of lingering drought. The sailor has been desperate to regain the wind that will finally move him forward from a powerless place on the lonely, still water. Oswald Chambers said: "Waiting for the vision that tarries is the test of our loyalty to God."[26] Frequently, our command is to wait. It is God's message to me so often that I suspect He is trying to make a point.

As you look for signs of God at work, you may hear a positive comment at a school conference. You might have one great hour of family time or a whole dinner without incident. Maybe you will see a tender act, or hear a gentle word from your child who has been a very angry soul.

I was amazed to write in my journal that, two months ago, my son and I stood in the kitchen and talked for an hour and a half straight. I cannot remember the last time that happened, if it ever did. A flash on the horizon, a quiet rumble of thunder far away or a ripple of air tousle a leaf upward from the ground. God is moving and God is causing movement. When you clean out a closet, you have to pull out all of the contents first, sort through them and slowly and methodically arrange them in their place. It's a mess for a while and it seems to take forever, but something is changing for the better.

A friend and I admitted that we have suffered through what seemed like extensive times of waiting on God, but other times God did something so fast that we were stunned. We concluded that God has the prerogative to do as He pleases at the pace He chooses. We may be sitting on the bench delayed indefinitely, or we may be swept away in the unforeseen wave of His speed. Who is to say how He will act?

Wait for it, watch for it. Thank Him for even a tiny shred of movement. "Be strong and let your heart take courage, all you who hope in the Lord." Psalm 31:24. This could be the day.

Thank You, Lord, for even the slightest progress in my child. Thank you that, if I don't see anything change, You are still working in my life, building faith and trust and loyalty in me. Thank You too that if I don't see movement with my eyes, You might be growing something under the surface.

Lord, I pray that You will move Heaven and Earth to draw my child to You. I pray that You will show me when to act and when to be still. Give me courage when I need to do something and patience to wait.

Day 55. Wide

"[B]ut just as it is written, 'Things which the eye has not seen and ear has not heard, and *which* have not entered the heart of man, all that God has prepared for those who love Him.'"

1 Corinthians 2:9

"Turn your eyes upon Jesus. Look full in His wonderful face. And the things on earth will grow strangely dim, in the light of His glory and grace."[27]

In my morning time with God, I prayerfully hand over to Him all of my concerns. Consistently it is the care for our son Ted. I leave my chair refreshed and more confident, knowing that God is in charge. Yet, at times, as soon as I leave that peaceful place I am drawn into a strong current of fears. Suddenly, I find myself thinking about what I must do to solve the problems that I have just turned over to God. I try to figure out, for the thousandth time, how I can help Ted in my own power. I squint to see a solution that has not presented itself in all of my prior attempts to think up a cure for the problem which is beyond me to solve. I forget that I have left this very trouble in God's capable hands to disentangle. In taking back the burden of my difficulties, I regain heartache because I forget that He loves me.

"I need to have Your eyes, Lord," I wrote in my journal. Jesus saw the world that He entered through the eyes of the Father. He was every bit in reality, but ensured, through His constant contact with God, that He viewed people and circumstances as the Father did. When I disconnect with God, I see reality through a lens of fear, failure or judgment. Sometimes, I even turn away from reality because I am not up to the challenge of dealing with it. Jesus confronted reality, and handled it head on, but always with a perspective of eternity.

Wide

I know if my mind could be quiet
A sound would come along.
Oh God, will You come calm the seas of
This lonely one, this one?

Show me the place where this life is just a day,
Show me the day where the past will fall away,
Come tell my eyes to be open, open wide.

To be wide. To be wide.

Remember the night that the storm raged?
You called out to me.
Remember when I said "not this time,
Stay away this time"?

God, I know You've been near the whole time,
But God, sometimes You seem hard to find,
These days my pride has been making me blind.

Show me the place where this life is just a day,
Show me the day where the past will fall away,
Come tell my eyes to be open, open wide.
To be wide. To be wide.[28]

Thank You, Lord, that my faith can handle my circumstances. Thank You for grace, what I need when I need it. Thank You for waiting for me to let go and being there when I do.

Lord, I pray that I could see my world as You see it. Help me to remember that this world is not as You intended it to be, but still You cause good to come from bad.

Day 56. Pecking Order

"If anyone comes to Me, and does not hate his own father and mother and wife and children and brothers and sisters, yes, and even his own life, he cannot be My disciple. Whoever does not carry his own cross and come after Me cannot be My disciple."

Luke 14:26-27

These two verses can be trouble for some people. The first one is alarming. You want me to hate my own family? I thought I was supposed to love everyone, especially my family.

Yes, that is true. We are supposed to love everyone, but sometimes our extreme love turns into a love that gets in the way of our love for God. God wants love that exceeds love for our children, our spouses or even our lives. He says that, if we love Him, we show it by obeying Him. This is love in action and not in word only. In comparison to our love for God, we hate everyone else. This is a radical illustration but, when you love God powerfully with your whole heart, mind and soul. By comparison, other love cannot compete.

Have you ever obeyed your child over what you know God would have you do? I have. I want to make peace. I want to keep my child happy. I want to loosen up and lighten up. I want my compromise to fix the problem so that it will go away. I want to be a fun mom, a cool mom. I want to avoid a confrontation.

When the need to obey God trumps what my child wants, fireworks often follow. Jesus says that it will cost us to follow Him.

The cost may be a turbulent, fractured or even broken relationship with our child. We love them desperately but we love God more. His Word to us is priority over anyone else's opinion, advice or experience. Our relationship with Him is our lifeline. We can't let anyone knot it up with their issues, expectations or demands.

I wrote in my journal about what it means to carry my own cross. Sometimes used as an excuse for self-pity, it isn't quite as dark a command as it appears. As usual, there's a good reason for what Jesus asks. When I carry my cross:

1. It is obvious to others. Let them see my relationship with God as my priority.
2. I am humbled by it. There is no servant, trailer or limo to carry it for me.
3. It reminds me of my purpose in life. It is easy to forget a gold cross around my neck, hard to forget a heavy wood cross on my back.
4. I better understand what God did to win me back from sin and death.
5. I can't hold much else in my hands when I am carrying a cross.

We carried our children inside us for nine months. A mother carried the adopted child in her heart until he or she reached her arms. We carried our children until they grew too big to be picked up, too resistant to be rocked, too strong to be restrained, too independent to manage. Long after our children walk without us, we still carry the cross of Christ in our arms for as long as we live. This commitment doesn't change or lessen.

St. Augustine wrote, "Love God and do whatever you want." Loving God first and foremost spawns a desire to obey Him, after which things have a way of falling into place. Sometimes we don't like where they fell into place but, if we are confident of God's love for us, they are as they should be. My relationship with God must come first or I am no good to my child in a crisis or to my family and friends.

Thank You, Lord, that the love You want from me is not on a par with the love I have for anyone else. I am honored that You even care how much I love You. I know that, when I spend time with You, I gain perspective on the rest of the world and I am at peace.

Lord, I pray that You will give me greater understanding of what it means to pick up my cross daily and carry it. Would You show me that this is a privilege and not a burden? Please give me an awareness that it may cost me, and let my cross symbolize extreme love.

Day 57. Not So Smooth

"By this is My Father glorified, that you bear much fruit, and so prove to be my disciples."

John 15:8

"I glorified Thee on earth, having accomplished the work which Thou hast given Me to do."

Jesus, in John 17:4

I cannot count the times I have asked God to cause some experience to go smoothly. Oh God, let this thing go exactly as I picture it as happening. Let everyone behave and send perfect weather. Please carry out every event without a hitch.

I think this was my prayer for the lives of my children when they were small. Let their lives go smoothly. Let my mothering go smoothly. Let my marriage go smoothly while the rest of my life goes smoothly.

I have observed, and continue to discover, that God is not preoccupied with making things go smoothly. He wants to point people to Himself and to be front and center in our lives. I have also noticed that my children's lives have not all gone smoothly, my mothering has not gone smoothly and my marriage has experienced jolts and shakes. Still, I can say that God caused good things to come into rough places. No one but God could have worked things out in those situations, and so He gets the credit and the glory.

Glory is one of those religious-sounding words that are seldom defined. Webster says it means "to light up brilliantly." The words honor, praise, admiration, and worship are also used to explain glory. Substitute those words for glorified in John 15:8 and see how the verse becomes more vivid. "By this is My Father lit up brilliantly, worshipped, admired, praised and honored, that you bear much fruit and so prove to be my disciples."

In His prayer in John chapter 17, Jesus summarized his brief time on earth by saying to the Father that He accomplished what He was sent here to do and that by doing that, He glorified the Father. No one could say that Jesus' life went smoothly. If anyone's should have, it would have been His. He did not sin. He knew everything. He loved people perfectly. He always said the right thing. He could do a miracle if He wanted to. At age thirty-three, however, He was nailed to a cross. That glorified the Father, but it was not smooth.

We point to God by the way we handle the imperfect things in our life, not by having perfect circumstances in our lives.

Some difficult things in my life and for my children and family are due to my mistakes. Some choices I made were not the right ones. But today, I ask God to work with what is, as it is, and make it what it should be.

> Ring the bells that still can ring,
> Forget your perfect offering.
> There is a crack in everything.
> That's how the light gets in.
>
> -- Leonard Cohen, Canadian writer

Thank You, Lord, for the awareness that nowhere am I promised that my life will go smoothly. I appreciate Your honesty in telling me that it won't. Thank You that You are in charge of all that does not go smoothly and that, in those times, I see my need for You.

Lord, I pray that You will take the rock-strewn places in my life and turn them into something that points people to You. Your life was not smooth, but it was fruitful. I want mine to be fruitful too.

Day 58. Three Keys

"And Jesus came up and spoke to them, saying, 'All authority has been given to Me in heaven and on earth.'"
Matthew 28:18

At our church senior high Mother's Day celebration, our youth pastor, Ryan, interviewed his own mom. After his parents' divorce, Ryan spent summers and holidays in another state with his father, who discouraged Ryan from pursuing his young faith. Ryan was prohibited from any church attendance or Christian activity when he lived with his dad. All his mom could do from a distance was to pray for her son.

In later years, Ryan experimented with the kind of behavior and activities that unsettle mothers. When he started college, he became disinterested in God and involved with a raucous fraternity. Although his mom talked to him about what better things God might have in mind for his life, Ryan continued in a different direction, away from following God.

His mom prayed on. When he went away to college, she could only pray. When he joined the fraternity, again she could only pray. Every day, she put Ryan in front of God and asked Him to get hold of his life.

In that freshman year of college, Ryan went to a Christian winter retreat against his wishes but in obedience to his mother. It was that weekend when his life swerved dramatically and his eyes were opened to change course and pursue a life with Christ.

In that Mother's Day service, Ryan asked his mom what she would say to the mothers in the audience. "I would tell you the three most important things to realize as a mom of teenagers are," she said firmly into the microphone as she counted on her fingers, one at a time, "One: never underestimate the power of prayer. Two: never underestimate the power of prayer. Three: never underestimate the power of prayer."

Are you in a situation in which your hands are tied, having said everything to your child that you have been allowed to say, or sense you should say? Are you a spectator, watching your child live life without God or any apparent influence for good?

Although He grieves with you, this might be just where God wants you. Speckled through scripture are all kinds of situations God shows us or Jesus tells us that change can only happen through prayer and prayer alone. God expects us to represent Him as best we can, but He does not tell us how to do what He does. We are never handed the keys to anyone's heart.

"Don't let this be my responsibility," I have often told God when I am confused by my child. "Don't expect me to bring about results. I have absolutely no idea what to do today, so I am going to do nothing," I have told Him. I believe that He would say to me, "Good. Thanks for letting Me handle it. Glad we had this little talk."

Never underestimate the power of prayer, the youth pastor's mother advised. That was all she had in her tool box but it was all she needed.

Thank You, Lord, that no one and nothing has authority over You. You are the first and last and final word. Your Word stands and Your way works. Thank You for prayer.

Lord, I pray that You will guide my child to the place and time where he encounters You. Grasp tightly to his life and unveil to him his need for You.

Day 59. The Bottom Line

"But now abide faith, hope, love, these three; but the greatest of these is love."

I Corinthians 13:13

A girlfriend called me to ask if I had any thoughts to pass on to another mom whose son was making some unwise choices as he began his high school career. I think my friend was expecting advice from me on how to curb his behavior before it got worse. Even I was surprised at my response, which concerned the behavior of the mother, not the son.

Less than an hour before, I had talked to a single dad I know whose son is a classmate of our son. It had been a while since we had talked. I called him because I knew the time was approaching when his son would be sentenced to jail time for another in a series of driving offenses. As I listened to Tom, I was touched again by the close relationship he cultivated with his son. The son's last violation would be life-altering but, having done all he could to direct his son rightly, Tom now just loved him. "We'll get through this," Tom told him.

When my friend asked for ideas for the wayward freshman's mother, I could only think of Tom's example. "Make sure her son always knows she loves him," I heard myself say. "Even when she doesn't like him, or he defies her, or she has to discipline him, or she's tempted to write him off, he needs to know that she loves him no matter what. If he knows that there is always love at home, then he knows there's a safe place to go when he is tired of himself. If she can't bring herself to say it, tell her to write it to him."

In all the head-butting that our son Ted and I did while he was in middle and high school, I feel I had not communicated my love for him often enough. However, I recall one evening as I kissed him goodnight, I said softly "If you never embrace what Dad and I believe or adhere to the morals we taught you, I will still always love you exactly the same as if you did." Somehow, I thought to solidify that my love was not conditional.

We know how hard it can be to show love when we are exasperated and discouraged. The father of the prodigal son did not condone what his son did, but he loved him through his foolishness and welcomed him when he returned home. The relationship was strained but not severed.

My husband is the toucher in our family. He reaches behind the driver's seat to grab a son's leg with a playful growl. He still calls his sons "honey" although they are bigger than he is, and insists on at least one long hug from them each day he sees them. He never lets go first.

Can your children admit without a pause that you love them? Even if they say they hate you right now and think you are pure annoyance, would they have to admit that they know you love them?

On the phone one summer day, my friend Annette made me think when she suggested I let down my guard and lighten up with Ted. "Put raisin eyes and a jelly smiley mouth on his toast," she said. "He's sixteen, Annette," I told her. "I know. That's the point," she said. "Stop being so heavy and have fun with him. It will break the tension." Annette offered other creative ideas to cause him to smile. I did some of those things and he responded in kind. Desperate for a connection, we found a simple start. To say it, show it, write it, prank it, love gets communicated if it's intentional. I am working on it.

Thank You, Lord, for putting love first. You say that You love me and You show it in a million ways. Thank You for giving me this child to love. Thank you for the endless chances You give me to change, and the way You keep working to make me be more like Jesus.

Lord, I pray that You, the creator, would inspire me to find ways to show and tell my child that I love him or her. Fill me with love when I am feeling empty. Remind me how much *I* appreciate Your love for me no matter how often I may disappoint You.

Day 60. Rock My World

"And He shall be the stability of your times, a wealth of salvation, wisdom and knowledge; the fear of the Lord is his treasure."
Isaiah 33:6

When the first of my three sons reached his teen years, I adopted this verse as my banner. I was moving from my familiar world of little boys to the rocky waters of adolescence and teenagers. Suddenly, I didn't have the last word in disciplinary exchanges. Situations about music, freedom, friends and activities cropped up for which I was not prepared. I worried because the whole thing took me by surprise and I was unprepared to face the new normal. How naïve of me. I had worked with teenagers and been one, but I expected my own kids to be different. With my expert parenting thus far, I thought they would stroll peacefully over this teen bridge into the land of happy, responsible adulthood.

The above verse lent perspective. Although this season of child-raising got shaky, God remained the same. He is stable. He is a resource. He planned the teenage phase. He's been one, and He understands them completely. That's good, because I think He is alone on that.

God is a wealth of salvation. Salvation is defined by Webster as:

1. Deliverance from the power and effects of sin.
2. Liberation from ignorance or illusion.
3. a. Preservation from destruction or failure.
   b. Deliverance from danger or difficulty.

Read those definitions again. God is rich and fully stocked in them.

He is a wealth of wisdom, something we cannot get enough of during the teen years. We can tap into the wisdom of others, to be sure. We can consult wise mothers with experience. We can talk to experts to help us zero in on issues. However, pure wisdom, tailored to our family and our circumstances, ultimately comes from God.

Now, and in the years to come, He is our stability. *On Christ the solid rock I stand, all other ground is shifting sand. All other ground is shifting sand.*[29]

Only our God is unshakable.

In 1989, my husband and I were at a business convention in San Francisco. We were talking in our hotel room while dressing for dinner when we suddenly felt the room tremble. "A train," I said, as we looked at each other. "No, an earthquake. Get down on the floor," my husband told me, and there we held hands and prayed for our two pre-school boys at home in Michigan.

In that moment I said to God, "I am ready to die, Lord, but I think I need to be here for my children. They're still so young." I decided that, if He did take us, our little boys would be all right. My soul was stable, even though the ground was not.

When our world is rocked physically, emotionally or with the onset of something new and different, God is still who He was yesterday and who He will be tomorrow. He was and is and is to come, unchanging. He is the solid foundation on which you can stand secure.

Thank You, Lord, that You are solid ground. Sometimes my knees feel like they are buckling under me and I need to grab onto You. Thank You that when everything is moving quickly and out of control, You steady me with Your wisdom and knowledge.

Lord, I pray that I would take You up on Your offer. I need You as my source of stability so I can be consistent for the people who depend on me. Make me a woman of wisdom with the knowledge I need to do what You want me to do.

Day 61. Scraping the Bottom of the Faith Barrel

"Sustain me according to Thy word (promise), that I may live; And do not let me be ashamed of my hope."

Psalm 119:16

We all probably know of an aged mother whose troubled son lives with her, unable or unwilling to live on his own. The mother takes responsibility for him and provides a comfortable environment, yet still expects him to grow up, beat his problems and mature.

Of course, I instantly personalize this type of story and worry that this could indeed be me at age 86, ever the victim, still waiting sadly while my son lives without God and steeped in unhealthy choices. This speculation opens the door to a type of panic that breaks into my heart to grab all the hope it sees and runs out with that hope in a bag on its back. I do not intend to have that future, but I still glom onto any extreme story and enter the land of "what ifs."

"Oh God," I say in my quiet time with Him. "I have about a mustard seed and a half of faith. You promise to work with that, but I would feel better if You poured some more into the barrel."

I open to the Psalms, which I know was written by others who like me, were at the top of teetering ladders, crying out for God to hold them steady. I come upon and read Psalm 19:16, quoted above, and search Webster's which tells me "sustain" means "to nourish, to buoy up, to bear up under, to support by adequate proof." I look up the word ashamed, "Feeling shame, guilt or disgrace. Feeling inferior or unworthy."

I want to be constantly aware of God's promises so that I can live out what God has for me to do in this life. I want to be leave something behind and make a contribution to the world, however small and to pass on even a fraction of the love I have received. I want the peace that comes from relinquishing control of managing the world and other people's business.

141

Forbid that I put my head down in embarrassment because I believed God would do something big. If God does not act in the way I expect, if He does not do things how I envisioned them to happen, I will not feel stupid for believing in Him. I have witnessed definite proof in my life that He can be trusted.

Our son John and I like to talk about song lyrics. We seem to particularly connect on ones that describe the attributes of God. When I listened to "I AM" by Lori Chaffer, I wondered how it is possible to lose hope in a God described this way:

> I am more than you think.
> I am more than you know.
> I'm as black as the darkest night
> And whiter than snow
> And I love you whether or not you believe Me.
>
> I'm as swift as an arrow
> But I'm slow when you stray.
> I'm as calm as the waters
> That we walked on that day.
> And I love whether or not you believe Me.
> If you ask Me again My reply still will stand,
> I am who I am
> And I love whether or not you believe Me.[30]

There are many things that are true about God which I negate when I become afraid. I compare my situation to another person's and assume the worst, as if there is no hope and God is restricted in certain circumstances. I cannot figure Him out. I cannot see into the future and I cannot predict His ways. I know enough about God to entrust my hope to Him and I will not be ashamed of it.

Thank You, Lord, that I know You would never allow me to be embarrassed because I trusted in You. Thank You that you understand betrayal of feelings and emotions and how they can, if we let them, deceive us into thinking You are anything but loyal to Your character.
Lord, I pray that you will allow me to concentrate on who You are when my heart races and I worry about what tomorrow holds. Fill me up with truth so that I am inflated with Godly confidence.

Day 62. The Whirlpool of Why

"I pray that the eyes of your heart may be enlightened, so that you will know what is the hope of His calling, what are the riches of the glory of His inheritance in the saints, and what is the surpassing greatness of His power toward us who believe.

Ephesians 1:18-19a

The weekend just ended has left me as discouraged as I have ever been. My communication with Ted was strained; he seemed impenetrable and I was on edge. He stayed away from me. He avoided conversation, but I could not think of anything to say anyway. His friend's widowed dad just died suddenly, and he is blaming God. I found myself somewhere between wanting to defend God to Ted and knowing that God is fully able to defend Himself.

I left a note for Ted, asking him to have coffee with me so that he could vent, if that is what he needs. While I was gone on errands later in the day, my husband talked with Ted in a pointed, direct and realistic way about who God is and what our options are when we wonder why God allows things to play out the way they do.

This morning, I sit wondering what to pray. My Bible is open on my lap. I page through it to find a chunk of wisdom, a wedge of encouragement, anything that will set me back on course. I want to get off my regular prayer merry-go-round and look at different scenery. I find fresh words to pray for Ted: "I pray that the eyes of your being will be enlightened." That's exactly what I want for him. I pray that the scales will fall off, the light will turn on. I want my son to get it. I want everything he knows and has heard about Jesus to come together for him.

My Bible has a hand-written note in the margin at Ephesians 1, that the word "heart" in verse 18 is synonymous with "being." I love the Apostle Paul's statement: "I pray that the eyes of your being may be enlightened."

Praying that request seems like a tall order in the face of Ted's sullen and angry attitude toward God at this moment. The rest of the passage reminds me that God is capable of filling the tallest order by His strength, might, power, authority, rule, dominion and absolute majesty.

I don't know why my son runs from God. I don't know how he began his diversion from Someone who has been a presence in our family since before he was born. How can Ted now ignore Someone we have loved, talked about and talked to, read about and served?

I know this happens. Diversion from God is all over the Bible in the prodigal son, the one straying sheep, the lost coin, and other parables and examples, but my best thinking tells me that, still, it should not have happened in our family. Yet despite my sincere efforts as a mom, my son has rebelled in a way that I never expected. Wasn't there a guarantee that, if you follow Jesus Christ in your home, your child's spiritual life will neatly fall into place? I naturally assumed that it would.

I, too, have asked the question my son is asking God regarding the death of his friend's only parent: why? Nevertheless, we are not promised that things will work out as they should in this life. As I ponder this issue again, I realize that I, too, need to review my responses when life is not fair. The coward of discouragement crouches behind the strong Jesus, but I willfully circumvent Jesus to confer with the coward.

When I was in college, we sang these words, which need to resonate in me today: "Open our eyes, Lord, we want to see Jesus, to reach out and touch Him and say that we love Him. Open our ears Lord, and help us to listen, open our eyes Lord, we want to see Jesus." When I stare at the bad situation, suddenly God is out of focus, in the background, or cropped out completely. He needs to be centered and in focus.

C.S. Lewis' words lend perspective: "I believe in Christianity as I believe that the sun has risen, not only because I see it, but because by it I see everything else."

Thank You, Lord, that I have choices. I can choose self-pity and angst or I can find peace in Your truth. Thank You that although much in this world does not make sense and is not fair, You remain the only One who sees the whole picture.

Lord, I pray that the scales would fall from my child's eyes so that he sees You clearly. I want him to know the hope of his calling, the riches of his inheritance in the saints, and Your surpassing greatness of power. Where I also am blinded by fear, let me see Jesus.

Day 63. Enter the Time Machine

"How great is Thy goodness, which Thou hast stored up for those who fear Thee, which Thou hast wrought for those who take refuge in Thee, before the sons of men! Thou dost hide them in the secret place of Thy presence from the conspiracies of man; Thou dost keep them secretly in a shelter from the strife of tongues. Blessed be the Lord, for He has made marvelous His lovingkindness to me in a besieged city."

Psalm 31: 19–21

At the end of a girlfriend weekend celebrating my fiftieth birthday, there were heart-to-heart talks all around the bus that drove eleven of us women back home. We were tired, introspective and vulnerable. The prior twenty-four hours of chatter had established a safe place to admit to a trusted friend sitting next to me, things that were somewhat muffled by the bus motor. "I don't really like being an adult," I heard myself confess to her, "I really don't."

I miss childhood, when I was ignorant of most evil, life was simpler, and I was oblivious to most other people's issues. I miss lying in bed thinking about Christmas and my birthday. I miss the days that slowly rolled into night without any to-do lists in my head. I miss the shallowness of being so excited to wear new shoes to school the next day that I couldn't fall asleep. I miss asking what we would eat for dinner, and finding the bathroom sink clean on Fridays without any thought or effort on my part.

I see my sons open a vacation day at noon and drift through the hours playing guitar or watching a movie, interrupted only by a phone call from a friend wondering what's going on that night. I want that to be my life again. I miss doing things because I want to, not because I have to. I wish people would keep their hard issues away from me so as not to tarnish my innocence and upset me. I wish I didn't know certain information about certain people.

I want to empty my mind of Mastercard bills and late fees, of registration deadlines and the helpless panic I feel about starving babies in Darfur and raped women in the Congo. I admit that I often long to lay aside the heavy responsibility of parenthood that I am feeling right now.

Jesus can relate. He was a child and then a teenager and then a man. His life got complicated. People with big issues latched onto Him. Some folks loved Him, but others ignored Him, some insulted Him and still others argued and left when He didn't say what they wanted to hear. He worried about people, individually and as a group. He wished that they would be reasonable and just let themselves be loved.

God gives us permission to be like children again. We are mandated by Him to be so humble, so vulnerable as to live our faith-lives as if we are children. He offers His fatherly protection as a haven from mean and difficult people who slap us with reality and push us down as we attempt to skip through life. We have to grow up and mature, but He does not forget that we sometimes want to be five years old and feel as though someone is taking care of us.

In verse 20 of the above passage, the word "shelter" is also translated as pavilion. A pavilion is defined in part by Webster as "a light sometimes ornamental structure in a garden, park or place of recreation that is used for entertainment or shelter." We can enter the shelter. He waves us in while He looks both ways for danger. He keeps the secret that we are hiding there. We have a place to escape not just to, but in, even when chaos surrounds us.

Can you go there? Jesus went there. Once it was in the garden of Gethsemane. The pavilion for Him was also up on a mountain, across the sea, in the streets of Jerusalem. It was and is everywhere God is. Your strong protecting Dad welcomes you as His little girl who is running from the paperwork and pressure, heartaches and bullies who are in pursuit. Be little for a time. Be the innocent who allows her Father to worry about the scary things. Go to the secret pavilion.

Thank You, Lord, that You welcome me as a child. If You didn't understand the heaviness that being an adult brings, You wouldn't bother offering to be my protective Father with a means of escape. I need You, God. I depend on You. Take care of me.

Lord, I pray that I can show others around me that I do not want to control everything, nor should I. Let them see how accepting I can be

147

of what comes my way, good or bad, because I trust and obey my Father.

Day 64. Soften

"'... I shall give them one heart, and shall put a new spirit within them. And I shall take the heart of stone out of their flesh and give them a heart of flesh, that they may walk in My statutes and keep My ordinances, and do them. Then they shall be My people and I shall be their God."

Ezekiel 11: 19–20

In this passage, God is speaking to the Israelites about returning them to their land, cleaning them up from the inside out and giving them a do-over. When I read this declaration of His intentions for those people, I can't help but raise my hand to say, "We could use some of that over here. Would you bring my child back to a good place? Take out the calcified heart and put in the soft one I used to know. Let the result be the same as You said in Ezekiel, a life-walk in obedience and closeness with You. Yes, that is exactly what I want for my own people, my child."

When friends ask how my son is doing in his second year of college, I am reduced to what I think is a good short answer: "He is softening." Softening is not a word I used much while praying for him during high school. I asked for things to stop or change. It never occurred to me to pray for softening. I should have, because things at that time were hard. Sharp words, blunt-edged body language, and attitudes like pumice rubbed everyone the wrong way.

In the last months he has said "I love you" and written caring words in birthday cards and spontaneous emails. The dreaded tattoo did indeed get etched on his arm. However, when balanced with his phone call from the dorm room to say, "I have to make some decisions about classes and I was wondering what you guys think," body art is incidental.

I wish I had been softer these last six years. Maybe I wouldn't have bruised him when he bumped into me. I might have been less dangerous to approach, and thus been approached more. How surprising to find myself responding to my kinder, gentler son. God has a way of coming in the back door when I expect Him at the front.

When you get in the bumper car with a challenging teen, you find yourself on a jerky ride in a closed-in space in which a defensive whiplash alternates with offensive collisions. What I had envisioned these years was rhythmic Ferris wheel ups and downs, until he stepped off the ride as a mature young man and walked off into adult land. In our real world of bumper cars, it seems as if the attendant has deserted us and the ride will never end.

Can we learn to appreciate it when the pace slows down, even slightly, and the atmosphere is more playful? Are we soft enough ourselves to recognize a vulnerable word from our teen that requires a gentle response?

I have prayed for a change in Ted's heart. I want fire to strike the ice cube, instantly changing it to a watery puddle in front of my eyes. Can I accept a slow thawing instead?

Only God knows where our son stands with Him right now. On this day I am surprised, humbled and thankful for that which I never thought to ask, a softening, in both of us.

Thank You, Lord, that You do the unexpected. That should not surprise me because only You know what is needed in each life. Remind me often of the way You orchestrated events, people and time to bring me to faith in You. I want to allow You the freedom to do things Your way in the life of my child.

Lord, I pray that You will soften me. Help me to relax in the knowledge of who You are and of what You are capable. Infuse me with grace for him, for others, for myself. Do for my son what You planned for the Israelites. I want my child to be one of those whom You call Your people.

Day 65. Account Manager

"Offer to God a sacrifice of thanksgiving, and pay your vows to the Most High;
And call upon Me in the day of trouble; I shall rescue you, and you will honor Me."

Psalm 50: 14, 15

While working for a real estate agent, I toured a teen rehab house and noticed this small sign in the kitchen window, "Good morning. This is God. I will be handling all your problems today. I will not need your help, so relax and have a great day." Not long after, my friend Jane gave me a laminated copy of the same saying for my window sill. Maybe that sign is cliché by now, but there is no better morning greeting when your feet hit the floor and your head recalls the problems of the new day like a computer downloading viruses.

In my morning devotion time, settled in my soft caramel-colored chair, I haul out the current issues of my life and put them on the proverbial table for discussion. Then God and I must decide who is handling what. If I am rational and choosing faith, I relinquish them all to Him.

Sometimes there are armloads of issue files, disorganized and neglected. Some mornings there is just one file, which I've reviewed and found to be beyond anything I can resolve, so He gets it. There is a different dog-eared file I've studied a hundred times and it begs for resolution, but I'm still trying to figure it out my way.

When God gets a file I do not see it again unless I demand it back. He does not promise me updates or progress reports. He gives me the option to put it back on my pile, which makes me overwhelmed and unsettled. Is control worth that, I wonder?

Recently, while my husband was traveling, I attempted to paint some china cabinets. When he returned, he offered to help me finish. At first I refused. I thought "I started this project and I want to do it myself," even though I knew my husband was a much better painter and if he did them, the cabinets would be flawless.

Later, I tired of the work and realized how ridiculous it was to be stubborn. I allowed my gracious husband to paint the last coat, well aware that, with his expertise, there would be no mistakes. Smooth surfaced cabinets that he paints are better than globby ones I do by myself. Why would I choose the worse result just to say I did it alone?

A young man told our church service the story of his recent life one Sunday. Jordan came from a close family and was raised with love by two parents, both of whom have a vital relationship with Jesus Christ. Jordan recalled that, from early on, he seemed to choose to do the thing that was opposite what he was supposed to do. At age 17, he was heavily into a heroin addiction and had been introduced to other drugs. By age 19, he was living on the streets, looking for ways to feed his habit. I was fascinated by what Jordan admitted: "I knew I could go to God, but I didn't because I knew if I did, He would help me. I wasn't ready to give it up."

George MacDonald, a nineteenth century preacher and lecturer, said "...the whole trouble is that we won't let God help us."

When my head is full of complicated problems, or I have a long list of things that unsettle me in the life of my child, I date my journal and write "God, today I need You to handle these things. As I write them down I ask for your complete management of the following," and I then list them one by one. At the end of the page, I thank Him for taking on the great and small so I can go out and live my day. When an alarming thing occurs in my life, it calms me to write down and pray about all of my fears associated with what just happened. Some people have a God Box in which they put their concerns on slips of paper for God to handle. They let go of them. When they open the box much later, they have often forgotten about the issues on the slips. He worked them out.

"I will be handling all your problems today," God reminds me. "I will not need your help. So relax and have a great day." That sounds like a plan.

Thank You, Lord, that what You want to do is to help me. It's all over the Bible. You wouldn't put me here without the power available to face what is terrible and confusing in my world. I am grateful that You are willing to shoulder what I cannot handle.

Lord, I pray that this day, one thing at a time, I give over to you that which visits my mind and troubles my heart. From a broken blender to a broken toe to a broken heart, I know You care. Would you remind me that there is a big picture of Your kingdom? I have a place in it, but it is not on the throne.

Day 66. A Good Handshake or a Shake-Up?

"For Thou dost not delight in sacrifice, otherwise I would give it; Thou are not pleased with burnt offering. The sacrifices of God are a broken spirit; a broken and a contrite heart, O God, Thou wilt not despise."

Psalm 51:16, 17

One of the things I admire about my son Ted is that he does not pretend. He, like most teenagers, is repelled by hypocrisy and would much rather not sing, pray, or speak using a spiritual facade if he is not engaged with God. If he's not doing it on the inside, he's not doing it on the outside.

I confess that it would make me feel better to at least occasionally see him go through the motions. Would I like that so other people would notice and admire the squeaky cleanliness of our model family? Or is it that I think that, if he went through the Christian motions, it would morph into devotion? Maybe both pride and hope contribute to what I long to see on the outside. What God longs to see doesn't start on the outside. Unlike me, He doesn't enjoy little actors and actresses putting on plays for Him. He wants me the way He meant me to be. I need to learn to want the real deal in my children and accept whatever they look like in the meantime. I should be more like my son in my disdain for hypocrisy.

As my college-age children mature, I have noticed what many parents have told me will happen. "They'll mellow. They'll like you more. They'll appreciate you more. They will outgrow the angst and the rebellion and become real law-abiding citizens whom you enjoy and who might even enjoy you."

I can see some of that. It's very pleasant. However, I want more for my children than that. My prayer has been for them to be all-out followers of Jesus Christ who boldly walk with Him for the rest of their lives. Author and speaker Brennan Manning says, "Jesus didn't die on the cross to make us nicer people with better morals."

"I want the farm," I told a friend yesterday about my desire for my children. "I don't want just well-mannered, I want the whole package." In his *Make it Real Jubilee Devotional*, Mel Lawrenz writes, "God doesn't merely want the thief to stop thieving. He wants to transform the thief's heart from greed to generosity. The cantankerous person should stop insulting and demeaning others, but needs to also look to God to put grace in his speech."

It is tempting to slow down or even abort our prayers for our children when they appear to be doing certain right things. Long periods in which they thrive can lull us into thinking that they are on their way, launched successfully and checked off. Don't settle for polite. Pray for God to lovingly craft them for a lifetime.

Thank You, Lord, for the commitment You have to make us new, not just nice. Thank You for the power You have to reach into a heart and work from the inside out.

Lord, I pray that You will perform a complete transformation in my son. Don't let me settle for good behavior in my dreams for my child. You are concerned with much, much more than that. We were bought with the price tag of Your life.

Day 67. Barely Believing

"Martha therefore said to Jesus, 'Lord, if You had been here, my brother would not have died. Even now I know that whatever You ask of God, God will give You.'
Jesus said to her, 'Your brother shall rise again.' Martha said to Him, 'I know that he will rise again in the resurrection on the last day.' Jesus said to her, 'I am the resurrection and the life; he who believes in Me shall live even if he dies, and everyone who lives and believes in Me shall never die. Do you believe this?'"

John 11:21-26

Martha is my new best friend. I feel today as though we are kindred spirits. I believe, but just barely. Martha called for Jesus but, in her estimation, He arrived too late. He could have saved her brother. No doubt, as the minutes ticked by, she was in a prayer frenzy about it, and yet Jesus did not come in time and her brother died.

Do you think she was disappointed? Can you imagine that her faith was not just shaken but fairly smacked down when she buried her brother? Yet, she was able to tell Jesus what she knew to be true, even though her heart was breaking and no one would blame her if she had gone home, pulled the shades, locked the door, crawled into bed and slept for days, too numb to cry.

However, Jesus does show up. He has a conversation with her. He talks to her sister, who feels the same despair and confusion. He acknowledges that the situation with his friend, their brother, is so very sad, but it is not hopeless. In the end, it comes down to what and in whom these two sisters believe. They are hanging onto truth, and yet their faith is encircled by the vultures of circumstance.

So it is with me at present. Is it with you? Do you feel like your faith is like an ocean wave that lifts high with power one day and then settles down into motionless complacency again for months or even years? You acknowledge that God parted the sea for His people once but inside you may be thinking "He doesn't do that kind of stuff anymore.

I believe He can, but I don't think He will. Frankly, the odds are against it."

In apparent hopeless times, I have said to God, "Maybe You don't change the minds of those who do not want them changed. Maybe you don't make over a heart that appears to be hard, cold or indifferent to You. Maybe if You did, that would contradict the gift of our free will. But once You parted the Red Sea. Once You raised the dead son of a woman on the street. Once You turned the water at a wedding into wine, in what I think is a much less desperate situation than mine. So please do something miraculous with my son, even one time in a way You have never done it before."

In her song, "Lord I believe in You"[31] Crystal Lewis sings, "Though I can't see You with my eyes, deep in my heart Your presence I find. Lord I believe in You. And I'll keep my trust in You." I play this song when I am running on the fumes of faith. Like Martha, I want to ask Jesus, "Where *were* You?" even though I know the truth and my experience shows me He is God no matter what happens. That truth and knowledge is enough to stand on. I choose not to believe my doubts. I choose to believe Him.

Thank You, Lord, that I know truth. In times when I don't feel much faith, I have promises and a history that keep me believing in You. Who knows what You will do and when? This is what I love about You, and also what makes me uneasy. It seems sometimes You are late or downright absent. I know that You are not.

Lord, I pray that You will keep putting courses on the walls of my faith. Let them be higher and sturdier so that, each time I must stand on them, I am closer to You.

157

Day 68. How? Now?

"And one of the synagogue officials named Jarius came up, and on seeing Him, fell at His feet and implored Him earnestly, saying, 'My little daughter is at the point of death...'"
"And after hearing about Jesus (the woman who had had a hemorrhage for twelve years) came up in the crowd behind Him and touched His cloak. For she thought, 'If I just touch His garments, I will get well.'"

Mark 5:22, 36

With my tendency to over-analyze, I wonder when I pray if I am asking Jesus in the right way. There are so many examples of how people ask Jesus for help, and just as many different ways in which He helps them.

A bold synagogue official named Jarius begs Jesus to come to his house and heal his sick daughter. A woman afflicted for twelve years with a hemorrhage does not have the courage to even speak to Jesus, much less look Him in the eye. She works up the nerve to touch His coat, with the hope that that will be enough to heal her. Both people are granted their requests.

In other Gospel stories, I see sisters Mary and Martha, with very different personalities, approach Jesus in different ways. I also read in Luke 7 how Jesus feels the heartache of a grieving mother whom He sees out of the corner of His eye. He raises her dead son without one recorded word from her. After reflecting on these examples, I abandon my search for a prayer formula.

I am also struck by the fact that Jesus did not heal these people when they first needed help. Why did the woman who touched Him live through a decade of suffering before the Savior came to her town? Why did the daughter of Jarius die before Jesus arrived? Wouldn't Jarius' faith have been sufficient for Jesus to heal her when she was gravely ill? Is Jesus acutely aware of the timing of events in our lives, or does He have complete disregard for time as we know it? I think the answer is both. He designed a universe in which time is a fundamental law but, as Creator, He can manipulate, respect, use or ignore it as He chooses.

Is it possible, in addition to the multiple mysteries of God's perfect intelligence, that Jesus cared more about the faith of these two people whose stories are recorded in Mark than how and when they experience healing? Jesus knew that Jarius would fall apart when he got word that his daughter has died, so He told him, "do not be afraid any longer, and only believe." He told the bleeding woman, who had every reason to believe suffering was her life-long destiny, "your faith has made you well."

Believe. Have faith. Know that Jesus has the power to undo and redeem the worst-case scenario. This is what I find, instead of a formula for prayer requests and an equation for answers.

Are you afraid when you think the time for an answer to prayer has passed? Do people in some way say to you, "Don't bother, it's already dead." Have you waited twelve long years or more for the Savior to come to the place of your situation and heal it? Maybe you have thought it's too late, that too much damage has been done, too much time has passed, or too much has been lost. That is also what some said immediately after the crucifixion.

Tenacious belief and stubborn faith are the answer to my how and when. I looked for a method and instead I got a mandate.

Thank You, Lord, that You use time as You see fit. You are not bound by the order of how things should happen. I love knowing that You are never too late. You feel no compulsion to hurry, but that does not mean that You are not fully aware of the hours and minutes of my life.

Lord, I pray for patience. Build trust into me as I see time slipping away. Sometimes I wonder what You are waiting for. Sometimes I grieve over lost years. Sometimes I think I cannot wait another day, and sometimes I hope that You have not forgotten about me. Just as I cannot control people, I cannot control time. You are in charge of both. "But as for me, I trust in Thee, O Lord, I say, 'Thou art my God.' My times are in Thy hand." Psalm 31:14-15a.

Day 69. Know Him or About Him?

"Not everyone who says to Me, 'Lord, Lord,' will enter the kingdom of heaven; but he who does the will of My Father who is in heaven. "Many will say to Me on that day, 'Lord, Lord, did we not prophesy in Your name, and in Your name cast out demons and in Your name perform many miracles?' "And then I will declare to them, 'I never knew you...'"

Matthew 7:22-23

There are no atheist mothers in the foxholes of their children's teenage years. This book is intended as a place where hurting moms can go to find encouragement in a lonely battle that needs constant faith and tenacity. So much is required of us in raising a teenager, and so much can be taken from us: self-esteem, time, social life, joy, other relationships and pride. What we thought we knew for sure is tested and can grow unsteady. A high-maintenance teen puts great pressure on our marriages and painful pressure on our hearts. I have invited you to walk the road with my God and me. This morning it occurs to me that I need to turn to you and ask you, do you know Him? Do you believe in Him and are you pursuing a growing relationship with Him?

Maybe you have someone in your life who would say she is your friend. She plans lunches with you, tells you everything on her mind, is pleasant and interesting, but you would not say she knows you. She has no idea what you think about life's issues big or small. She doesn't know about your children or childhood. She doesn't know how you live, what you care about, the things you value or what wisdom you have. She talks and you listen. Is this how you are with God? He knows you. Do you know Him?

I respected and admired a certain president. I knew some things about him personally and even more about him politically. I worked very hard on his campaign. I told others good things about him and supported his views. I went to rallies and appearances. I helped him get elected. We would never say, however, that we knew each other.

At one time in my life, I was this way with God. I respected and admired Him but I would not say we were friends.

Do you listen to God by reading what He has to say to you in the Bible? Do you listen to Him in prayer, being sensitive to the still, small voice He might cultivate in your thoughts as you pray? Are you interested to know what Jesus did, what He taught and said? Do you involve Him in every aspect of your life, not just in the struggles with your teen? Do you thank Him and share your happiness with Him? Would you say you love Him with all your heart, mind, soul and strength or that you want to? Most importantly, would you say that you believe that He loves you?

If you are not sure, I applaud your honesty. Please understand that you *can* know Him. You can be confident that He is in your life to stay and you will be with Him and He will be in you, now and through eternity. 1 John 5:11-13 says:

> And the witness is this, that God has given us eternal life and this life is in His Son. He who has the Son has the life; he who does not have the Son of God does not have the life. These things I (the apostle John) have written to you who believe in the name of the Son of God, in order that you may know that you have eternal life.

When I arrived at college my freshman year, I would say I loved God but thought I wasn't the Christian type and therefore not eligible for God's inner circle. For that reason, I discarded the possibility that He and I would ever be close, although I suspected there was some link to Him which I missed along the way. My roommate then told me that God wants a personal relationship with everyone, which is why He made us. I didn't have to be a certain personality type for His acceptance. He takes me as I am.

Once I understood that I could know the God who loves me, I considered it for a while, and then made the decision to turn my life over to Him. One night in February, 1976, I knelt by my dorm bed and asked Jesus Christ to forgive my lifetime of sins and come into my heart. I needed Him to take away my guilt and give purpose and meaning to my life. I gave Him permission to make me who He wanted me to be.

162

Anxiously but resolutely, I told Him He could have my future to do as He wished. If He really was who He said He was, then I could trust Him. Then I thanked Jesus for dying in my place on the cross, and said amen.

I have never looked back. For 31 years, He has been my friend and Savior. He has never disappointed.

I want this for you more than any comfort or companionship this book might offer. You will find everything you need in Him. If somehow these words can point you to Christ, I urge you to say yes to Him and begin your eternal friendship today.[32]

Thank You, Lord, that You want to know us. We can barely begin to appreciate the gift of a growing, lifelong relationship with the living God, still, it is ours for the asking. Thank you for making forgiveness possible and offering a life of purpose and meaning as it was meant to be.

Lord, I pray for the reader who knows You, that her relationship with You will continue to grow deeper and sweeter. For the reader who does not, I pray that You will help him or her to hand over a me-managed life to the One who is waiting to fill it with Himself.

Day 70. The Persistent Parent

"...and He who searches the hearts knows what the mind of the Spirit is, because He intercedes for the saints according to the will of God."

Romans 8:27

When I pray for our son to live his life walking with Christ, I often picture the reality the Bible tells us of God on His throne in heaven with Jesus at His right hand. Jesus is the intercessor, asking and pleading for us. Webster's defines an intercessor as the one who presents a prayer, petition or entreaty in favor of another. Every day, and through the day, I remind God of my request. I picture Jesus resting on his elbow, leaning toward the Father's ear, and saying "It's Sarah again... about her Teddy."

God knows the details. He's heard them ad nauseum. The idea is always the same, to draw Ted, let him realize this very day the depth of Your love and respond to it.

My friend Cindy often ends her emails to me by saying that she is the persistent widow on my behalf. In Luke 18, Jesus is talking to His disciples and tells them a parable, "to show that at all times they ought to pray and not to lose heart." Unlike God our Father, the judge in the parable does not care much about the actual petition of a widow who asks for legal protection against her opponent. However, because the widow is relentless, the judge gives her what she requests.

"Even though I do not fear God nor respect man," the judge says, "yet because this widow bothers me, I will give her legal protection, lest by continually coming she wear me out." "Hear what the unrighteous judge said; now shall not God bring about justice for His elect, who cry to Him day and night, and will He delay long over them?"

If God could be worn out, I am making that my job. I know that my prayer is in His will, so I boldly forge ahead.

This month I am reading in I Timothy, Chapter 2:3-5 which says,

This is good and acceptable in the sight of God our Savior, who desires *all* [emphasis added] men to be saved and to come to the knowledge of the truth. For there is one God, and one mediator also between God and men, the man Christ Jesus, who gave Himself as a ransom for all, the testimony borne at the proper time.

Sometimes I feel sorry for God as my friends, our family and I continue asking, asking, asking Him to rescue Ted. I cannot stop because I know the Christian life can be hard to live, but it is the only way to live; God in you, God with you, God for you. We can stumble through the dangers of life in darkness and disorientation toward an uncertain end, or walk through the dangers of life in light, with confidence and hope, assured of heaven with an almighty God who loves us. I vote for the latter.

We are tempted to lose heart. At times I have come close, but after a while, I am ready for discouragement to leave. I don't like it nearly as much as taking heart.

Pray and don't lose heart. Ask and ask and ask again. When you come to Jesus for the two thousandth time, He can be depended on to lean into the Father to say, "it's his mom again and You know what she wants." God does not think I am a nag. If He didn't want me to ask Him, Jesus would not have said to keep up the campaign. I'm submitting my signed petition today, and I'll be there again tomorrow. I hope you will be too.

Thank You, Lord, for encouraging me to knock at Your door. I fully intend to stay there. Even as You hold the planets in Your palm and oversee the universe, You listen to me and work out Your plan in my life. In that I am encouraged. I take heart.

Lord, I pray for staying power. Let me not lose heart or if I do, let it repel me so that I return to Your doorstep. It is good that You don't tire of my requests because I won't stop until my son turns to follow You. It's me again, Jesus. You said I could come.

Day 71. The Offer on the Table

"And I, if I be lifted up from the earth, will draw all men to Myself."

John 12:32

I have spent the summer lingering in the gospels, one at a time, to see what I can find. I try to remember to ask God to show me something fresh or new or relevant to my day. Along the way, I always discover something else that is incredible about Jesus.

Today I continued in John, chapter 12. I stalled on verse 32, where at some earlier time I had circled the word "all." I will draw *all* men to Myself, Jesus said.

Earlier in John 6:44, Jesus tells the Jews "No one can come to Me, unless the Father who sent Me draws him; and I will raise him up on the last day." This verse has prompted me to pray hard this summer, "God, draw Ted to Yourself."

The thought that God might be choosing to draw some and not others could have left me feeling uneasy. I decided that I would not dwell on the not-picking part, but pray that my son will be in the draw camp. Still, as an over-thinking person, the mystery and question of being drawn or not bothered me.

In chapter 12, Jesus says that He draws ALL men to Himself. The choice bounces back to us. Free will is the loving gift God gives to human beings, but in that gift lies a decision to accept or reject Him. Therein is the wild card that haunts me.

So I circle back to the fact that many people do not choose Him. They say no to the offer of abundant and eternal life. I can only pray for my child. Why does he stay away from God?

I have been on both sides of the fence. As a teenager, I behaved in a way that left me ashamed and empty. I was thirsty for something I could not name. While I exercised the freedom to be in charge of my life, I did not like who I was becoming. Then my college roommate explained that I could know God personally. I wanted that.

166

God gave us the opportunity to throw out the life preserver to our son on several occasions. He sent signals that he was unhappy and discontent with his present circumstances, friends and state of mind. We offered the rescuing power of Jesus, but he continues to bob up and down, breathlessly treading water. There is not anything else I can offer him. All other life-saving devices have holes in them. Because I love him, I will keep watch with the life preserver, but I cannot force it over his head. I will not leave the edge of the boat or turn a deaf ear to his cries, but my answer will be the same as it has always been. You cannot save yourself. God can. Do you want to let Him?

God does His part because He so desperately wants us. He loved us first. He chooses us first. He draws men and women to Himself. He died to make a life with Him possible. He rose again to show us He can do anything. The work is done. We can choose the gift by our surrender and acceptance. The only thing He does not do is make up our mind for us. If God can wait for Ted to do that, I can too.

Thank You, Lord, that You have already established everything we need to be saved out of the deep and turbulent waters of this life and the darkness of eternal life without You. Thank You for this place of prayer, where I commit the free will of my child to You.

Lord, I pray that You will complete my child. As he grows tired trying to stay afloat on his own, let him grab onto You.

Day 72. The Extra Mile

"So we fasted and sought our God concerning this matter, and He listened to our entreaty."

Ezra 8:23

In her Bible reading time, a friend came across the verse quoted above, and thought I might be interested. She knows there seems to be a spiritual tug-of-war going on in our son Ted's life and, although I want to, I cannot think of a way to pray more intensely. She suggested that I fast.

This summer, Ted and I made a pact. He would give up smoking and I would give up the candy and desserts I love very, very much. Based on Cindy's suggestion, I added a fast of chips and soda pop. My son was quitting for his health but, although I know it is good for me to have less sugar and salt, I intended this as a fast in prayer for him rather than a healthy eating plan. I had no problem with chips and soda, but it was disturbing to me how intensely I missed sweet things. Ted cut back his smoking and I reduced my treats, but neither of us had complete success for the whole summer.

In times of crisis, I have fasted meals and certain foods that are very dear to me. Fasting heightens the intensity of my communication with God and is a reminder of my dependence on Him. I want to be sure He knows I am serious. I am rewarded by knowing that He hears my entreaty, my earnest request, as Webster puts it. I am ashamed how hard it is for me to sacrifice a dessert for someone I love. Jesus offered His life, but I struggle to give up an unnecessary pleasure. I am needy so I pray and, when that doesn't shout loud enough for me, I fast. I sacrifice a tiny thing so I can remember what He has done for me, even death on a cross, and ask Him for that which I can never do myself.

Thank You, Lord, that You are bigger than anything I know. I try to make You fit my design but You never do. Thank You for wanting me to seek You in things that concern me. You will listen.

Lord, I pray that when I fast, You will give me the very small taste of what it means to sacrifice for something you want very, very much. You wanted me and You sacrificed your life. As I remind You of my prayer when I fast, remind me that you are a God who listens.

Day 73. Testing or Trusting

"Be anxious for nothing, but in everything by prayer and supplication with thanksgiving let your requests be made known to God. And the peace of God, which surpasses all comprehension, shall guard your hearts and your minds in Christ Jesus."

Phillippians 4:6, 7

I was alone in my car, loudly venting to God with tears running down my face and into my lap. I thought, but was afraid to ask Him out loud, why in the world do I bother to pray? A dozen people for whom I regularly pray seem to show no change in their lives—in fact, their circumstances are getting worse. I thought maybe I should take a praying hiatus, as an experiment to see if my prayers make a difference. Then I thought of myself, "how arrogant."

In his book, <u>Blue Like Jazz</u>, Donald Miller writes,

> Many of our attempts to understand Christian faith have only cheapened it. I can no more understand the totality of God than the pancake I made for breakfast understands the complexity of me. The little we do understand, that grain of sand our minds are capable of grasping, those ideas such as God is good, God feels, God loves, God knows all, are enough to keep our hearts dwelling on His majesty and otherness forever.[33]

I don't understand exactly how prayer "works." How much is enough? What is God's method of operation in deciding how and when to answer prayer? Do we really change God's mind and the course of human history through our prayers? These things are interesting to explore, but not possible and perhaps not necessary to grasp. What I know about God tells me that I can trust Him with what I want, so I will. I'm going to keep praying that my son will walk with God one day and, when things get worse, I will fast.

I don't see everything I pray for come true within my own deadlines. Still, I keep praying and try to throw away my prima donna parameters, demands I make like a spoiled princess who stomps her foot until she gets her way. Sometimes I'm not sure exactly what prayer is, but I know it's not that. I know that God says to ask Him, talk to Him and listen to Him. He says to not grow weary, pray without ceasing. He says that, if it is in His will, I will receive that for which I have asked. I also know, as more than a footnote, that I have already received thousands of answers to prayer, and many more of my prayers have been answered or perhaps noticed although I have not witnessed the result.

I am connected with God through prayer. God and I forge a relationship when we talk. I read what He says in the Bible and He promises to help me understand it by His Spirit in me. He listens to me. His Spirit in me directs me as to how to act, if I listen to Him.

My husband tells of the many after-dinner hours that he spent in the basement of his childhood home with his father as he did moonlighting work. As a young boy, my husband would sit on a stool next to his father and chatter on about his thoughts and the events of the day. His father would listen and affirm all the ideas that fill the mind of a young boy. He addressed the worries with wisdom. Those times bonded the two of them and shaped much of my husband's character.

In the same way, I trade thoughts with God and an attachment occurs. I don't have to evaluate or measure the outcome of that exchange. The fact that we have such a tender relationship is enough. "Have you been asking God what He is going to do? He will never tell you. God does not tell you what He is going to do; He reveals to you who He is."[34]

Thank You, Lord, for the mysterious gift of prayer. Thank You for deepening of our relationship through this constant communication. My prayers do change things, but how and when are in Your hands.

Lord, I pray that I not concentrate on how prayer works, but on how it helps me know You better. The better I know You, the more secure I am in trusting You for all that befalls me and those I love. My heart settles down when I trust You.

Day 74. Resolutions

"'Of old Thou didst found the earth; and the heavens are the work of Thy hands. Even they will perish, but Thou dodst endure; and all of them will wear out like a garment; like clothing Thou wilt change them, and they will be changed. But Thou are the same, and Thy years will not come to an end.'"

Psalm 102:25-27

Have you noticed how often people do not keep their promises? When I was a girl, my father periodically told our family that his drinking days were over. In the end, he didn't stop drinking until it was too late. The alcohol claimed his life at age 56. I remember where I was standing the last time my dad told me he was done with drinking. "That's good," I told him. "We'll see," I told myself.

At various times, people have declared to me that they are, from this day forward, changing their way and starting over. Some resolutions have come to pass, but many have not. I know enough that I should be skeptical, but often I believe and rejoice, only to be disappointed when the person does not keep his or her word. Sometimes I even blame God that people do not follow through. I accuse God of pulling my strings like a marionette and then dropping me on the stage floor in a heap of despair.

I have felt as though God messed with my head when my son has announced that he wants to follow God and then it doesn't happen. Things continue on as they were. I feel naïve, like a child who keeps packing for Disneyland only to have the offer repeatedly withdrawn. I have made my own resolution that, the next time someone I love declares a seismic change; I will not allow myself to count on it until I see it.

In my resolution not to be callous or cynical, I remind myself that peoples' promises are not God's promises. Imperfect people realize that change is necessary, but often lack the power or conviction to follow through. A person's recognition of the need to change is a balm to those who hope for them and wait. When I resolve to do things

172

differently, sometimes I do and sometimes I do not. When I am wise, I ask God to change me according to what He intends, not what I promise. I am grateful He has the power to do it.

I wish I knew the appropriate response when someone we love makes a promise that we have longed to hear. In Psalm 103 and Psalm 104, I see a rock-solid God who is incapable of weakness and in Him only do I trust. Can I grant others the same grace and forgiveness I would like from them? Their progress is not for me to measure. I will trust in the Rock that is higher than me.

Thank You, Lord, that Your promises are true forever. You don't change. You don't waver. You are my rock. You are dependable, solid ground under my feet. You never disappoint.
Lord, I pray that You will direct me in how to handle disappointment. Teach me to give others the benefit of the doubt and the encouragement they need. Let me not invest my trust in people, but in You. Help me give them the grace you give to me.

Day 75. Epilogue

"Paul and Barnabus appointed elders for them in each church and, with prayer and fasting, committed them to the Lord, in whom they had put their trust."

Acts 14:23 NIV

Ted went through six months of residential treatment for drug and alcohol addiction in the fall of 2008. He has since told us that he began his experimentation with substances 10 years before, when he was 11 years old. Years ago, when I could see that he was headed in the wrong direction, I wrote this in my journal:

> Lord, last month I committed Ted to you (again) to stay away from harmful influences. He is vulnerable. He wants to be near some kids I don't care for.
>
> I know he recognizes right and wrong but his fascination with cool can be stronger. A few weeks ago I was sad and scared about this. I was driving down Bluemound Road telling You this fear and saying, "God, you have to take care of him. Some things are beyond my control." My eyes moved to the right on the road and I saw a car's back license plate. It simply said, "TRUST."
>
> I see how You love me Lord. You reassured me how you have Teddy in the palm of Your hand. Now Lord, as many are praying for him, you have tugged him up again when he slipped, reeling him in and I am comforted for awhile, fully expecting to hold him up in prayer the rest of my life – which is my privilege and security.

Little did I know that God would take us down the road of the devastation of substance abuse for the next decade. I was right to be afraid and it was right to trust Him. If Ted's addictions were not beyond my control at the beginning, they most certainly were by the end. I had no idea they were so severe. I just knew that things were very bad and the dark cloud above us was not moving. Still, I trusted.

My husband and I did everything we could think of to help Ted, but there was so much we did not know. Some things we did not want to know and some we ignored because...I'm not sure why.

God kept His grip on Ted during those ten years. At the right time, all who had prayed for him (and there were many) saw their prayers answered above and beyond what we could ask or think. Ted has been drug and alcohol free for two years and loves God fiercely. He has a wonderful Alcoholics Anonymous sponsor who helps him work a recovery program as he lives life with God as his strength and power. Now a senior at Augsburg College in Minneapolis, Ted lives in a dormitory dedicated solely to students in recovery. He is a resident assistant; has been awarded a scholarship by his college for academic achievement, exemplary character and leadership; and is living the life of his dreams while also serving others. He has given his blessing to the writing of this book.

Until just over two years ago, I was either unaware of Ted's addictions or denied them, and perhaps both, if that is possible. I have learned since then that no one can serve two masters, God and addiction. I thought that Ted's only problem was that he stubbornly refused to acknowledge God and say yes to Christ. I thought that a personality gone awry was responsible for all the bad behaviors he practiced. It was more complicated than that, or maybe simpler, but I did not understand the whole picture. I probably never will.

Still, the heartbreak of a child who leaves the bonds of one's family, whether emotionally, physically, or socially, is the same whatever the cause. What I wrote in my journals for that decade was what God showed me about trusting Him. Those things sustained me and gave me hope. My prayer is that you will find the same.

During Ted's time of trouble, I took on his problems and made them my own. I lost a lot of myself in those years of sadness and worry. When Ted was in treatment, his counselor strongly suggested that I attend Al Anon meetings.[35] I did. With the help of my Al Anon sponsor, I began to work my own 12 step program, and learned that God has a plan for my life apart from Ted's or anyone else's issues.

The father celebrated when the Biblical prodigal son "came to his senses" and returned home. Our family is still celebrating Ted's return. Life is not perfect, but now our family is united. I am aware that many, many families are not complete, and that some never will be. Every single night I give thanks for, among many other things, another day of Ted's sobriety, knowing that God guarantees nothing about our futures except that He will never leave us or forsake us.

I do not know if Ted would be in a relationship with God if he had not experienced the chaos of those years. Maybe that was necessary for him. In my life, that difficult time forged an attachment between God and me that I might not otherwise have known. In spite of the acute pain of that period, I am amazed by what God built from it.

A friend asked me to start a substance abuse branch of her Christian wellness organization. I learned about addiction, drug use and alcoholism, particularly in adolescents. This of course helped me better understand Ted's battle and that of my late father. Eventually, I joined forces with Your Choice,[36] a substance abuse education, prevention and awareness program for students and parents. I tell my story, with the prayer that it might help someone. For this privilege and the many good things that have come from that dire place, I am deeply grateful.

"If through a broken heart God can bring His purposes to pass in the world, then thank Him for breaking your heart."[37]

Endnotes

[1] Jeremiah 33:2-3 (New American Standard Bible). Unless otherwise stated, all references in this text are to the New American Standard Bible.

[2] Isaiah 40:31.

[3] Nichole Nordeman, "Glory" recorded by Selah, *Bless the Broken Road: The Duets Album,* [compact sound disk], copyright 2006, Curb Productions, Inc. Nashville, Tennessee.

[4] Fernando Ortega "I Will Praise Him, Still," *Fernando Ortega – Hymns of Worship,* [compact sound disk], copyright 1998, Word Music.

[5] James 1:4.

[6] BeBe Winans, "Stand," *Freedom*, [compact sound disk], copyright 2000, Motown.

[7] Psalm 142:3a.

[8] Oswald Chambers, My Utmost for His Highest (Dodd, Mead & Company, Inc. 1990), p. 45.

[9] Steven Curtis Chapman, "Believe Me Now," *All Things New*, [compact sound disk], copyright 2004, Sparrow Music.

[10] James Taylor, "Shower the People," *James Taylor Greatest Hits*, [compact sound disk], copyright 1976, Warner Brothers.

[11] Ruth Bell Graham, Prodigals and Those Who Love Them (Baker Books Grand Rapids, MI 1999), p. 5.

[12] Damaris Carbaugh, "Is There Anything Too Hard for the Lord?" *Heart Mind and Soul*, [compact sound disk], copyright 1998, Discovery House Music.

[13] Ibid.

[14] Lamentations 3:22, 23.

[15] Lyrics by Reginald Heber, melody by John B. Dykes, "Holy, Holy, Holy," 1826. Published in *Hymns Ancient and Modern*, 1861. Copyright NICAEA.

[16] "Intercede." *Webster's New Collegiate Dictionary,* 1973.

[17] "Sovereignty." *Webster's New Collegiate Dictionary*, 1973.

[18] Oswald Chambers, My Utmost for His Highest (Dodd, Mead & Company, Inc. 1990), p. 186.

[19] "Bulwark." *Merriam-Webster's Collegiate Dictionary, Eleventh Edition*, 1994.

[20] DC Talk, "Fearless," *Supernatural*, [compact sound disk], copyright 1998, Forefront Records.

[21] Steven Curtis Chapman, "I Believe in You," *All Things New*, [compact sound disk], copyright 2004, Sparrow Records.

[22] Cheri Fuller, When Mothers Pray (Multnomah Publishers, Inc. 1997).

[23] C.S. Lewis, Mere Christianity (Harper Collins Publishers 2001).

[24] Lyrics and music by Jeromy Deibler, "Lord Move or Move Me," *FHH Found a Place,* [compact sound disk], copyright 2000, New Spring Publishing, Inc.

[25] Chris Tomlin, Shawn Craig and Jesse Reeves, "Mighty is the Power of the Cross," *Arriving,* [compact sound disk], copyright 2004, CMG Publishing Worship Together (see Worshiptogether.com).

[26] Oswald Chambers, My Utmost for His Highest (Dodd, Mead & Company, Inc. 1990), p. 71.

[27] Helen H. Lemmel, "Turn Your Eyes Upon Jesus," *Glad Songs,* The British National Sunday School Union, Public Domain 1922.

[28] John Nielsen, "Wide," recorded by The Cloud Hymn, *A Seed Buried in the Ground,* [compact sound disk], copyright 2009, Amble Down Records (see Ambledown.com).

[29] Lyrics Edward Mote, melody by William B. Bradbury, "The Solid Rock," 1836. First published in Mote's *Hymns of Praise.*

[30] Lori Chaffer, "I AM," recorded by Waterdeep, *Sink or Swim,* [compact sound disk] copyright 1997, Hey Ruth.

[31] Crystal Lewis, "Lord I Believe in You, *More* [compact sound disk] copyright 2001, Tommy Walker, Doulos Publishing / BMI.

[32] For more information about how to know God personally, go to www.Everystudent.com.

[33] Donald Miller, <u>Blue Like Jazz: Nonreligious thoughts on Christian Spirituality</u>, (Thomas Nelson Nashville, TN 2003).

[34] Oswald Chambers, <u>My Utmost for His Highest</u> (Dodd, Mead & Company, Inc. 1990), p. 2.

[35] Al-Anon shows the friends and family of alcoholics and addicts how to live their lives with serenity, whether or not their loved ones are still drinking or using. Alcoholics Anonymous is for alcoholics; Al-Anon is for us. I find the program to be invaluable. To find a meeting near you, call 1-888-4Al-Anon (1-888-425-2666) or visit www.al-anon.alateen.org.

[36] Your Choice is a program developed by parents of a son in recovery from addiction. Young adults share their personal experience about the devastation on their lives from alcohol and other drugs, or about their choices to stay drug-free and found reward. To learn more about Your Choice, visit www.YourChoice-Live.org.

[37] Oswald Chambers, <u>My Utmost for His Highest</u> (Dodd, Mead & Company, Inc. 1990), p. 306.

CPSIA information can be obtained at www.ICGtesting.com
Printed in the USA
LVOW082127071011

249659LV00001B/131/P